Let the debate ... ier
that Terry is

MW01061551

GREAT DETROIT SPORTS DEBATES

Peter,
Enjoy the Debates AND
we Are in one THE Best.
Sports Towns In America

DREW SHARP
VS.
TERRY FOSTER

Terry Foster

SP
SPORTS PUBLISHING L.L.C.

SportsPublishingLLC.com

Photos courtesy of the Detroit Free Press
Cover illustration: Mark Anderson

Publishers: Peter L. Bannon and Joseph J. Bannon Sr.
Senior managing editor: Susan M. Moyer
Acquisitions editor: Mike Pearson
Developmental editor: Elisa Bock Laird
Art director: K. Jeffrey Higgerson
Cover design: Heidi Norsen
Interior layout: Heidi Norsen
Imaging: Heidi Norsen
Photo editor: Erin Linden-Levy

Printed in the United States of America

Sports Publishing L.L.C.
804 North Neil Street
Champaign, IL 61820

Phone: 1-877-424-2665
Fax: 217-363-2073
SportsPublishingLLC.com

Library of Congress Cataloging-in-Publication Data

Sharp, Drew.
   Great Detroit sports debates / Drew Sharp versus Terry Foster.
      p. cm.
   ISBN 1-59670-048-3 (softcover : alk. paper)
   1. Sports—Michigan—Detroit. I. Foster, Terry. II. Title.

GV584.5.D6S43 2006
796.09774'34—dc22

                          2006001889

To my late parents, Calvin and Donna Sharp, who told me
that I was a know-it-all who should have a newspaper column
since I had an opinion about everything.
So what if I was only nine.

—D.S.

I must honor the women who raised me even though
two of them are no longer with us.
This is dedicated to my grandmother,
Fannie Mae Ratliff, and my aunt,
Margaret Louise Sherman, who told me to
look beyond my boyhood boundary of Livernois, Tireman,
and Grand River. And thanks to my cousin, Juanita Purifoy,
who acted as a big sister and went through life as "Miss
Boots" because I have a habit of giving everybody nicknames.
Thank you to my mother, Betty Foster,
who continues to give moral support.
And much love to my family: wife, Adrienne, and children,
Celine and Brandon, who bring much joy and love to my life.
I also love the passionate sport fans of Detroit. We've
battled and we've agreed. But many of you were always there
for me during the ups and downs of my journalism career.

—T.F.

Contents

ACKNOWLEDGMENTS   vii
INTRODUCTION   viii

SECTION 1:   Motor City Musings   1

Is Detroit a baseball or football town? 2
Will we see the Lions' first Super Bowl before another
    Tigers' World Series? 5
Who is the ultimate captain of a Detroit sports team? 8
What's the best nickname in Detroit sports? 12
Name the top three Detroit sports moments from
    the first half of the 20th century. 16
What's the best logo in Detroit sports? 19
Name the top three Detroit sports moments from
    the second half of the 20th century. 21
Name the three best trades in Detroit sports. 25
Name the three worst trades in Detroit sports. 29
If the United States Senate possessed the power
    to impeach one person in Detroit sports, who would that be? ... 33
Who was the most overrated player in Detroit sports? 37
Name Detroit's three all-time sports characters. 41
Who is the biggest opposing villain in Detroit sports history? 43
Name Detroit's top three good guys in sports. 46
It's generally agreed that the first three faces of granite on Detroit's
    Mount Rushmore are Joe Louis, Gordie Howe, and Isiah Thomas.
    But who deserves the fourth spot—Al Kaline or Ty Cobb? 49
Who was the most underrated superstar in Detroit sports? 52
What's the best classic uniform in Detroit sports? 56
Who is the most influential woman in Detroit sports? 60
Name the top three all-time Detroit sports jerks. 63
What's the tougher job in Detroit sports—Wings' goalie or
    Lions' quarterback? 66
What was the biggest gamble ever in Detroit sports? 69
What was the biggest blunder in Detroit sports? 72
What movie title would you give each of the four professional
    sport franchises and why? 75

SECTION 2:   Grid-Iron Gridlock   79

Who had the biggest impact on football in the state of Michigan? 80
Who was the best player in college football in the state of Michigan
    who should have won the Heisman? 84
Who's been better for Michigan football—Bo Schembechler or Lloyd Carr? ... 87

Who was Michigan's best No. 1 in football? 91

Did "Spartan Bob," the timekeeper, hose Michigan in its 2001 loss
    to Michigan State? 94

You are starting a new Division 1-A college football program in the state
    of Michigan. Do you want Lloyd Carr or John L. Smith taking
    the reins? 97

Will Wayne State ever become a Division II college football power? 101

Would Detroit gladly trade its recent professional and collegiate
    championships for one Lions' Super Bowl win? 104

Who would you take—Barry Sanders or Billy Sims? 107

As the Lions coach you are down four points with two minutes left.
    Which quarterback—post-Bobby Layne—do you want under center? ... 111

What was the most dramatic Lions touchdown? 114

Who was the worst Lions' draft pick? 117

Who was the best big-play player in Lions history? 120

SECTION 3: Hardwood Head to Head   **123**

Who was the better Pistons coach—Chuck Daly or Larry Brown? 124

Who was the most important Pistons' first-round draft pick? 129

Who is the best Pistons sidekick? 132

The Pistons scheduled a press conference for Isiah Thomas to make
    him a Piston for life, but it never happened. Why? 135

Could Tom Izzo coach an NBA team to the world championship? 138

There's one opening on the Pistons' all-time starting lineup, which already
    includes Isiah Thomas and Dave Bing in the backcourt, Bob Lanier at
    center, and Dennis Rodman as one forward. Who do you pick to fill
    the last slot? 141

Who would have won a best-of-seven series between the 1989
    and 2004 Pistons? 144

SECTION 4: Skating Around the Subject   **149**

Who is the real face of the Red Wings—Steve Yzerman or Gordie Howe? ... 150

The Wings have won three Stanley Cups in 10 years. Why? 154

Terry Sawchuk is the greatest Wings goalie ever. But if there was a Game
    7 of the Stanley Cup finals, which other Wings goalie do you want in
    the net? 156

Could a second NHL team survive in Detroit? 159

Who scored the biggest goal in Red Wings history? 162

It is generally agreed that Terry Sawchuk, Steve Yzerman, Gordie Howe,
    and Nicklas Lidstrom belong on the Wings' all-time starting six.
    But who should be the left wing and the second defenseman? 166

Who was the Red Wings' biggest Original Six rival? 169

SECTION 5: Rawhide Rips   **173**

Who would have won in a best-of-seven Series between the 1968
and 1984 Tigers? 174

Who would join Ty Cobb in center and Al Kaline in right as the left fielder on
the all-time Detroit team? 177

Who was your all-time Tigers catcher? 180

Who had the best season ever for a Tigers closer? 183

Who is your all-time Tigers second baseman—Charlie Gehringer or
Lou Whitaker? 186

Do Alan Trammell and Lou Whitaker belong in Baseball's Hall of Fame? 189

In a Game 7, which Tiger do you want on the mound—Mickey Lolich
or Jack Morris? 192

Who deserves the next statue at Comerica Park? 196

What was the most memorable/dramatic Tigers' home run ever? 198

Will Alan Trammell's unsuccessful stint as Tigers manager ruin his long-term
reputation as a player? 201

What was the most dramatic All-Star Game home run in Detroit history? 203

Which Tigers manager could Detroit best identify with—Sparky Anderson or
Billy Martin? 206

It's the bottom of the ninth, the bases are loaded with two outs, and Detroit
is trailing by one. Which Tiger do you want at the plate? 209

SECTION 6: The Buzz about the Brews, Brats, and Buildings   **213**

Which rivalry is better—Michigan versus Michigan State or Central Michigan
versus Western Michigan? 214

Which Michigan school has the best college football game day experience? 217

What facility best defines the Red Wings? 220

Name the top three all-time radio/TV broadcasters. 222

Where should the potential new home for Red Wings hockey go? 225

The city of Detroit has sold its soul for one glorious day in sports.
What would that day entail? 227

Which place was better to watch a ballgame—Tiger Stadium
or Comerica Park? 229

What should happen to Tiger Stadium? 231

What was the best feature of Tiger Stadium? 234

After Detroit, what is the best sports city in the state of Michigan? 236

The Grand Prix has been held in downtown and on Belle Island.
Which was better? 239

Could Detroit host a Summer Olympics? 241

Name the top three all-time Detroit sports bars to watch a game if
you don't have tickets. 243

Acknowledgments

We thank the *Detroit Free Press* for its cooperation in granting us access to its photo library, with special appreciation to director of photography Nancy Andrews and photo department clerk Gina Brintley for their valuable assistance. And we salute staff photographers Kirthmon Dozier, Julian Gonzalez, Amy Leang, Mary Schroeder, Eric Seals, and Susan Tusa whose work appears in this book. It is through their eyes and imagination that the great moments in Detroit sports forever live in our hearts.

Introduction

TERRY ON DREW I met Drew Sharp during my first week of working at the *Detroit Free Press* in 1982. He'd just graduated from the University of Michigan, and we became part of a young nucleus that emerged into some of the best sportswriters in America.

Johnette Howard (columnist at New York *Newsday*), Clifton Brown (*The New York Times*), and Tommy George (*The New York Times* and *Denver Post*) all left the *Freep* and worked in New York. Drew and I became columnists in our hometown. We became good friends, and that bond grew when we became Pistons beat writers at competing papers. I moved to *The Detroit News* in 1988, and we both covered the Pistons during the 1989–1990 championships.

Drew used to be mild mannered, but he grew into an agitated lion when he felt his turf was being invaded. This was never clearer than the time I knew he was my boy. We were on a tight deadline during a game at Chicago Stadium, and I was seconds from sending in my story when a Chicago radio reporter snatched my phone. I told the selfish scribe to give it back. He didn't. So I snatched the wire from the back of the phone during his report. He threatened me, and I said as soon as I was off deadline we could finish this. Drew turned, cursed the guy out, and then threw a full cup of Coke and ice in his face.

Security was called.

Two days later, I called Drew's hotel room in Milwaukee.

"Hey, 'Boodini', I think we are in trouble. Our fight made the *Chicago Tribune*."

The paper said the Pistons were not the only Bad Boys from Detroit. The paper called us "The Bad Boy" writers.

We have a lot in common. Drew was born in Ypsilanti, but we both grew up on the west side of Detroit, loved Detroit sports as kids, celebrated the 1968 Tigers' World Series, and worked briefly at the *Grand Rapids Press*.

He is a graduate of Detroit Catholic Central (1978) and U-M (1982), but claims the university revoked his diploma because of his rips on the athletic program. And, by the way, he is also hated by Michigan State, the

Big Ten, most Detroit sports fans, old ladies who sit in the bleachers, and most of society.

Whenever my radio partner Mike Valenti is on vacation, I ask Drew to fill in. I know we can disagree, argue, and not hold grudges.

I gave him his nickname "Boodini", because Drew was wrong on everything. But during a one-month period he nailed everything. It was like magic. So I combined the names of the magician Hoodini with former Muhammad Ali trainer Drew "Bundini" Brown.

I am happy to see him spread his wings and do his thing in the newspaper and on ESPN. He's worked hard. I always root for my homies. When I pitched this project to him, he enthusiastically got on board, and I am honored to do this book with him.

May sales be as brisk as your rips of the Big Ten, my friend.

DREW ON TERRY | If I had a dime for every time I was confused for Terry Foster or he was confused for me, I could live a richly subsidized retirement comparable to that of a Lions' first-round draft choice. The confusion is understandable, because our lives have closely paralleled each other.

We both were raised on Detroit's west side, although I've long had difficulty finding the exact place where Terry lived. He has steadfastly maintained that he grew up in the "house of respectability," but unfortunately, the white pages offer no such address.

What immediately struck me about Terry was his passion, a willingness to metaphorically incorporate sports within the inconsistencies and injustices of life. Some people frown upon that. Sports should remain separate from real life, but Terry has always understood that "real" people participate in sports, so why not draw parallels.

Passion is a necessary component for discussion. That's why our collaboration for this debate book was inevitable.

Rarely have we agreed on anything during our numerous arguments over the years, discussing the merits or flaws of teams, players, and coaches over brews and Buffalo wings on the road after a game.

But our disagreements never required security guard intervention until a Pistons trip to San Antonio in January 1991.

The Lions were hosting the Dallas Cowboys in a NFC playoff game at the Silverdome. Terry believed the game symbolized a seismic course alteration for the long-suffering Lions, but I just categorized it as one of those unexplainable flukes like the occasional Democrat taking up residency in the White House.

As the Lions rolled on to a big victory over the Cowboys, our words morphed into other forms of whimsy—like a hotel room wrestling match.

"Say it, 'Boodini!' Say it!" Terry demanded with my head vise-locked in his arms. "The Lions are a solid team! Say it!"

"Never! They still suck!" I managed to mutter.

"I'm not letting go until you say they're solid!"

"Never!"

A half hour later, we got a call from hotel security. The person in the room below wondered what the hell was going on overhead. Either we were to tone it down, or we risked expulsion from the Marriott Riverwalk. Or maybe they threatened to toss us into the Riverwalk.

It's taken 15 years, but I think Terry finally realized that I was right all along about the Lions.

MOTOR CITY MUSINGS

 Is Detroit a baseball or football town?

DREW | There's a stronger connection to baseball in Detroit because there's a deeper history. The Tigers have been here for 105 years now. They are one of the charter members of the American League. They weren't born elsewhere and moved here like the city's other professional sports franchises.

And don't tell me about how Detroit might react to the Lions winning a Super Bowl.

We know how the city has reacted to tight pennant races in September and successful World Series runs in October.

Detroit exploded—in a positive way.

There's a generational bond with baseball in this town that football can't replicate. Terry, if it were possible, you and I could sit with our fathers and grandfathers today and each could share in what it was like getting a daily adrenaline fix from the Tigers' world championship seasons of 1935, 1945, 1968, and 1984. Football reaches its climax on one day after a week of buildup, but nothing compares to the emotional ebb and flow of a stirring baseball season, because it could change daily.

And that's why the Tigers' fall from respectability has been more insulting personally than the Lions' championship difficulties, because if you were born after October 1987, you would have graduated high school before seeing the Tigers return to the playoffs.

TERRY | I do not play or work for the Detroit Lions. But it is impossible for me to go to dinner without some poor schmuck walking up and saying: "What's wrong with the Lions? How can we fix this team?"

This town is obsessed with the Lions even during this pathetic five-year 21-59 stench under president Matt Millen. The Lions dominate the airwaves, the sports talk shows, and the minds of the fans.

If the Lions ever won a Super Bowl, the parade route would stretch from Pontiac to downtown. And every inch of space would be filled with people even in the dead of winter. That is how much the Lions mean to people.

When the Tigers lose, nobody cares. When the Lions win, lose, scratch, burp, or fall down, it becomes front-page news. Ford Field is filled every Sunday with more than 60,000 fans who start out thinking this is the year the Lions finally make the Super Bowl and leave with blue and silver face paint smudged from tears.

> "When the Lions win, lose, scratch, burp, or fall down, it becomes front-page news."

And I didn't even mention the 112,000 people who show up in Ann Arbor for Michigan football and the 72,000 who venture to East Lansing to see Michigan State play. The high school scene is popular, too. Football fields are filled every fall as people await annual battles between Grosse Pointe South and Grosse Point North.

People's lives revolve around fall.

Michigan fans walk around with a sense of entitlement. Their lives rise and fall on the fortunes of the Wolverines. Paranoid Spartans fans carry around lucky rabbits' feet hoping this is the year they finish better than 5-6 or 6-5. They complain about their teams constantly. But guess what? They are there every Saturday tailgating and cheering their teams on.

The Tigers lost an entire generation of fans. Ask anybody under 20 about the Detroit Tigers, and they will point toward the Detroit Zoo in Royal Oak. The biggest day in summer is Opening Day at Comerica Park, and it is all downhill for baseball from there.

The second biggest day is the opening of Lions' training camp. After that folks only think football because by then the Tigers are an afterthought in the American League.

# Will we see the Lions' first Super Bowl before another Tigers' World Series?

DREW As pathetic as Lions management remains and as determined as they are in magnifying mistake upon mistake, the Lions are still more likely to get to the Super Bowl before the Tigers get back to the World Series because the NFL system is manipulated toward parity. The vast financial disparity in Major League Baseball still has significant influence in determining the better teams, placing even more pressure on the front offices of the lower revenue franchises. They have a much smaller margin for error in baseball than is the case in the salary cap-driven NFL.

The odds are better for the Lions because the chances of making the playoffs are greater. Teams with 8-8 records have made the NFL playoffs five times since 1999. The lowest winning percentage for any baseball playoff team during that same period was the San Diego Padres in 2005, winning the National League West Division with an 82-80 record.

Consider the last 10 Super Bowls and World Series as of the fall of 2005: There have been 14 different teams participating in the Super Bowl, including six teams that got there for the first time. There have been 13 different teams participating in the World Series during that time span, but one team—the New York Yankees—participated in six Fall Classics. And it isn't a coincidence that the Yankees have consistently had the highest payroll in baseball during that period.

You can't dismiss the realities that money is equal in the NFL. Yeah, it's blatant socialism in that the bigger cities and media markets are no better financially than the smallest—little Green Bay, Wisconsin, and its population of just more than 120,000. But the NFL understood that the key to everybody flourishing is fostering a sense of optimism in every city that their team just might have a chance to win it all, if a few things fall the right way.

And I suppose that's even possible with the Lions. Not likely—only possible.

But that beats the mess that's become the Tigers.

TERRY | Normally I would agree with Drew that the Lions have a better chance than the Tigers. But with the divisional format the Tigers do not have to worry about beating the large payrolls of the New York Yankees and Boston Red Sox until the playoffs. The Tigers could get swept by both teams the entire year, still make the playoffs, and win the World Series.

The Tigers must only beat the Chicago White Sox, Cleveland Indians, Minnesota Twins, and Kansas City Royals. That's it.

The great thing is all of these teams must maintain moderate spending levels. They are not going to compete with the Yankees and Red Sox in spending.

But who won the World Series last year?

It was the White Sox. And haven't we seen the Arizona Diamondbacks (2001), California Angels (2002), and Florida Marlins (1997, 2001) win World Series in recent years?

The Lions are run by Matt Millen, a guy who has ruined this franchise. They won't win a thing as long as he is in charge. Heck, they may not even reach .500 under Millen.

Tigers general manager Dave Dombrowski at least has a track record. He can go into a room full of front-office executives and not hear snickers. Millen cannot say the same. Dombrowski put the 1997 Florida Marlins together and is well respected in the baseball world. He loves power pitching and understands that that is the way you get to the playoffs and the World Series.

The Lions are still trying to figure out how to hire a head coach and draft a quality quarterback. You can talk about NFL parity. But if you do not have a good coach and quarterback, you are not winning a title.

Consider this fact. Since 1968 the Tigers have won two World Series. The Lions have won one playoff game since 1957.

Now if the Tigers win their division, anything can happen in a playoff series. The best team does not always win in baseball because all you need are two quality pitchers and timely hitting to win a series. The best teams usually win playoff series in basketball and football. Baseball truly is a sport when one team can win on any given day.

That is why the Tigers will be the next team from Losers Lane to win a championship.

**Who is the ultimate captain of a Detroit sports team?**

DREW The title of captain carries a lot of weight in a blue-collar town like Detroit. And what best defines the blue-collar mentality is toughness.

Mateen Cleaves and Antonio Smith were the first of the "Flintstones," Michigan State's basketball pipeline connecting Flint to East Lansing. They were co-captains during the 1999 season when the Spartans took their first steps to becoming a nationally elite basketball program, earning the first of four Final Four trips in a seven-year span, including the national championship in 2000.

Cleaves and Smith, who both came from Flint Northern High School, were the ultimate captains—good players who demanded great things.

Smith was Izzo's first recruit, a power forward with vise-grip hands. He wasn't the best jumper or the biggest player. He just wanted the ball more.

Smith took charge as a freshman, immediately following a tough loss at Purdue. The Spartans' captain that year, senior Jon Garavaglia, had laughed off another road defeat. Outraged, Smith grabbed Garavaglia, dragged him into the showers, slammed him up against the wall, and yelled at him, "I didn't come here to lose!"

The message was clear. A new day had arrived for Michigan State basketball.

Could two college kids (Mateen Cleaves, pictured, and Antonio Smith) be *the* captains of Detroit sports?

Izzo likes guys who play football because he believes they possess a greater emotional reserve than other athletes. Given the right circumstances, they can draw upon that resource. Smith was a high school tight end. Cleaves was an All-State quarterback in high school.

The right circumstance for Cleaves was halftime of the 2000 NCAA Tournament Midwest Regional semifinals at The Palace of Auburn Hills. The No. 1-seeded and heavily favored Spartans trailed Syracuse by 14 points. They played undisciplined and uninspired—especially Cleaves's childhood friend, forward Morris Peterson.

Cleaves chewed out his good friend in the locker room, challenging his toughness.

Peterson came out on fire in the second half, scoring 16 of his 21 points, as the Spartans won, scoring 17 unanswered points over the game's final six minutes.

When asked afterward what triggered that performance, Peterson said he didn't want Cleaves kicking his butt had they lost.

TERRY | Drew!! You picked two kids as the ultimate team captains in Detroit sports? You had your choice of Steve Yzerman, Ben Wallace, Gordie Howe, and Alan Trammell, and you went with a pair of college students?

Who was your second choice? The captain of the Regina High School powder puff team?

Now here is the real team captain of Detroit sports.

In spring 1990, the defending NBA champions were in a slump. Team captain Isiah Thomas thought his front line was playing soft, and he wanted more fire.

The day after one of those losses, I entered the team's dressing room to find a lone figure in front of his dressing stall. Thomas sat with his feet soaking in ice water as a million demons swam through his head. When I approached him, Thomas ripped into the play of James Edwards, John Salley, and Bill Laimbeer. He demanded more of his big men. If they didn't have the muscle and hustle to do a better job, he said Pistons general manager Jack McCloskey should trade for someone who would. Shortly afterward, the slump ended, and the Pistons captured their second NBA title.

Thomas didn't always go about things the right way. He angered teammates and ruffled a lot of feathers in the Pistons organization.

But where would the Pistons be without him?

They'd be the Detroit Tigers in shorts.

When a player came to the Pistons, he had to face Thomas, the gang leader of the Bad Boys.

For example, when Rick Mahorn was traded to the Pistons in 1985, he met with Thomas and Laimbeer in a dressing stall at the Pontiac Silverdome.

Laimbeer looked at Mahorn with disgust and said, "You're fat."

Mahorn looked pleadingly at Thomas, hoping the captain would come to his defense.

"He's right. You are fat," Thomas said.

Thomas learned his tough management style from his mother, Mary Thomas, who raised nine children alone in a tough neighborhood on Chicago's west side.

One night, gang members came to her home looking to recruit Isiah. She pulled out a sawed-off shotgun and screamed, "There's only one gang here, and I lead it. Get off my porch, or I'll blow you off it!"

Thomas guided the Pistons to three NBA Finals as well as championships in 1989 and 1990.

He also led by example. Thomas's 16 points in 94 seconds against the New York Knicks in April 1984 and the Game 6 classic of the 1988 Finals against the Los Angeles Lakers rank as two of the best performances in professional sports history. In the L.A. game, he scored 25 points in one quarter. That still stands as an NBA Finals record.

What's the best nickname in Detroit sports?

DREW | The perfect moniker was born inside the imagination of Lakeland Tigers' pitching coach Jeff Logan in 1974 when a young, gangly, curly-headed, right-handed pitcher from New England joined the Detroit Tigers' rookie league organization. The pitcher possessed the free spirit of a child, so Logan equated him with a children's television character.

And Mark Fidrych became "The Bird."

Logan thought Fidrych resembled the beloved *Sesame Street* character, Big Bird.

The Tigers entered the 1976 season as an easily forgettable team. They were a year removed from a 102-loss campaign, which was then the second-worst season in the franchise's history. There wasn't much hope for improvement.

Fidrych was the last pitcher added to the 25-man roster. But little did anybody know that such an innocuous personnel decision would ignite the Year of the Bird.

Notable nicknames now inspire a boxer's brute strength like "Iron Mike" Tyson or an agile quarterback's elusiveness like the Denver Broncos' Jake "The Snake" Plummer.

But the name "The Bird" had nothing to do with Fidrych's approach to pitching and more to do with his approach to life. Fidrych was a free spirit, unfazed by the sudden scene that swept him into the national sports consciousness in the summer 1976. He was like a kid in his free flight, just enjoying the ride and not concerned as to where it might take him.

Fidrych's career was a blink. He was an emergency starter May 15 against the Cleveland Indians at Tiger Stadium. Who was this kid with the quirky mannerisms? Is he talking to the baseball? What's he doing on his knees manicuring the mound at the beginning of each inning?

But more importantly, he took a perfect game into the fifth inning and had a no-hitter through six innings before surrendering a leadoff single in the top half of the seventh inning.

Fidrych won the game 2-1, and a bland team suddenly possessed a personality that soon captivated the country.

Fidrych won 19 games that season, earning American League Rookie of the Year honors. He pitched 24 complete games, unheard of with today's more specialized pitching roles. Four of those complete games were shutouts.

He was named the American League starting pitcher in the 1976 All-Star Game at Philadelphia.

But, more importantly, "The Bird" made the game fun. Fidrych gave birth to the modern-day baseball curtain call. Fans, who flocked to Tiger Stadium to watch "The Bird" take flight that summer, refused to leave the stadium long after the game ended until they saw their hero once more. Fidrych sauntered back onto the field from the locker room, all smiles and in aw-shucks amazement.

But, unfortunately, Fidrych's arm couldn't keep up with his aura.

The rotator cuff in his right shoulder was gradually tearing away even then. Fidrych injured his arm in training camp in 1977, missing the first two months of the season. He was welcomed back to action with a *Sports Illustrated* cover, sharing the stage with his namesake—Big Bird.

It was Fidrych's last flirtation with the spotlight.

TERRY | Joe Louis chose the nickname "The Brown Bomber" because he considered it the least offensive of the monikers created for him, such as "The Shufflin' Shadow," "The Tan Tornado," or "The Dark Destroyer."

"The Brown Bomber" was perfect because it acknowledged Louis's place as one of America's first black superstar athletes. The name also described the fury with which he knocked out German boxer Max Schmeling in their 1938 rematch. Louis bombed Schmeling, whom German chancellor Adolf Hitler held up as model of Nazi Aryan superiority.

> **"[Joe Louis] loved being 'The Bomber' because it showed his power."**

Joe Louis Barrow was one of 16 children, a merger of two families.

My aunt, Margaret Sherman, and grandmother, Fannie Mae Ratliff, knew the Barrow family. They often talked about how Louis was so humble and nice outside of the ring. But when the boxer hit the ring, he became a different man.

Aunt Margaret once told me that Louis was proud of his nickname. He loved being "The Bomber" because it showed his power. He was the heavyweight champion from 1937 to 1949, the longest reign of any single boxer ever in any single weight class.

But he was proud of the Brown part, too.

That generation grew up in a time when "negroes" were kept down, called names, and attacked by whites. Louis was proud of his heritage, and he loved the support he got from the black community. He fought for all of America, but he fought especially for blacks, whom he knew would never abandon him.

Ironically, we almost never got to know "The Brown Bomber." At age 16, Louis used violin lesson money to rent a locker at Brewster

Recreation Center in Detroit. His mother, Lillie Barrow, was furious when she discovered he was boxing. But she relented and encouraged him to pursue his dream. His only association with music after that was hanging out with jazz musicians Duke Ellington and Cab Calloway.

After his death in 1981, President Ronald Reagan authorized his burial in Arlington National Cemetery, waving eligibility rules that require military battle experience for interment.

That's the kind of respect this country had for his fighting ability and his example as a leader.

Name the top three Detroit sports moments from the first half of the 20th century.

DREW   **No. 1:** Joe Louis avenging the lone loss of his career when he knocked out Germany's Max Schmeling in two minutes and four seconds of the first round of their historic fight on June 22, 1938. My parents told me of how everything stopped in Detroit whenever Louis fought, but never more than on that day. They were kids, but they hovered around the nearest radio with their families. It was the eve of World War II, and Louis's dominance leveled a symbolic punch to Adolf Hitler's Nazi Germany.

No. 2: Jesse Owens wasn't sure if he would be physically able to compete in the Big Ten track and field championships in Ann Arbor on May 25, 1933. He had injured his back, falling down a flight of stairs just days before the meet. But he convinced his Ohio State coaches to let him compete in the 100-yard dash. He tied the world record with a time of 9.4 seconds. Obviously healthy, Owens entered the 220-yard dash, 220-yard hurdles, and the long jump—and set world records in all three events in a matter of 45 minutes.

No. 3: The New York Yankees' Lou Gehrig was the game's "Iron Horse," having played a record 2,130 consecutive games. But that streak ended in Detroit on May 2, 1939, when Gehrig was too ill to take the field against the Tigers that afternoon. He never played again. Gehrig didn't know that he was dying. He was soon diagnosed with amyotrophic lateral sclerosis, or what has come to be known today as Lou Gehrig's disease. Gehrig died on June 2, 1941.

T E R R Y | Drew, I loved your three moments. But I am going to introduce three more.

No. 1: The Tigers played their first American League game on April 25, 1901, and Detroit officially became a baseball town. The Tigers were one of the charter members of the new major league, and they had the biggest ballpark. Bennett Park was constructed five years earlier at the former site of a haymarket. After an expansion in 1901, it could seat more than 10,000. Bennett Park would experience many more additions as well as name changes. It went from Bennett Park to Navin Field to Briggs Stadium to finally Tiger Stadium in 1961 when broadcasting magnate John Fetzer bought the franchise. Detroit's baseball history is secure in that it was home to the oldest baseball facility on one site. The Tigers played at The Corner for 103 years.

> **"Today, not just Detroit, but the entire nation plans its holiday around Lions football."**

No. 2: Detroit became the City of Champions during an eight-month stretch beginning in autumn 1935 when the Tigers won their first World Series. All three of the city's sports teams won their respective league championships at the same time. The Lions won their first NFL title on December 15, 1935, when they defeated defending champion New York Giants 26-7. Running back Ernie Caddell led the Lions in both rushing and receiving yards that season. The Red Wings completed the triple crown when they defeated the Montreal Canadiens in the 1936 Stanley Cup finals.

No. 3: The Lions' first Thanksgiving Day game in 1934 began one of the NFL's great traditions. When R.A. Richards bought the Portsmouth Spartans, he moved the franchise from Portsmouth, Ohio, to Detroit and renamed them the Lions. Richards thought the name complemented the Detroit Tigers. But he needed something to help his football team stand out, so Richards petitioned the league to host the first Thanksgiving Day game. The Lions played the Chicago Bears. Today, not just Detroit, but the entire nation plans its holiday around Lions football. It became such a big deal that other teams sought to change the league rules and rotate the Thanksgiving Day game between a number of teams. But the NFL refused to take the game away from Detroit. This was Detroit's baby, and without question its biggest contribution to professional football.

# What's the best logo in Detroit sports?

TERRY Can Tom Selleck, Snoop Dogg, and Tupac all be wrong?

They all wore the Tigers' Old English D on baseball caps and jerseys. The symbol is easily identifiable. When you wear a cap with the Old English D, it's not necessary to tell anyone where you're from. They already know. Having Selleck wear the cap on his TV show, *Magnum P.I.*, in the 1980s was a great source of local pride.

Detroit was kicked around a lot during the 1980s with national attention on Devil's Night fires engulfing neighborhoods and one of the higher murder rates in the country. So it was nice to see a nationally recognized celebrity employ the Tigers symbol to show the nation that it's cool to support Detroit.

Unfortunately, the logo is more popular than the team.

The Red Wings and Michigan football have enjoyed far more recent success. Fans love the winged wheel on the Wings jerseys and the ram's horn or flames or whatever the image on the U-M football helmet represents. The helmet design helped the team stand out on the field during games, and former Michigan running back Jamie Morris told me that he fell in love with the school because he saw the helmets on TV.

I suppose the Red Wings logo is OK. But let's be honest. It is a tire with feathers coming out of it. It is classic, but silly at the same time.

Drew, here is our agreement. The next time you see Snoop or Selleck wearing a Red Wings cap on television, you win your argument. The problem is you will never see it. The Old English D is where it's at.

DREW | Who's kidding whom? Can it be anything but the winged wheel?

The Detroit Cougars began play in the NHL in 1926 but struggled financially and competitively. Relief arrived six years later when grain-millionaire and shipping-magnate James Norris bought the franchise and wanted a fresh start.

Norris recalled his teenage days when he was an amateur hockey player in Montreal for a team called the Winged Wheelers. And their logo was, of course, a winged wheel.

Thus the name "Red Wings" was born.

The logo hasn't changed one bit in more than 70 years.

I love logos created within the abstract. People look at the Wings uniform and try to decipher what the logo means. It's a wheel, right? So that must symbolize Detroit's association with the automobile industry. And the wing must represent speed, right?

It's hard for people to understand that the winged wheel possesses no subliminal meaning. The owner of the team simply liked the design.

A logo can mean anything—even if it isn't consistent with its original intent.

Yet, the winged wheel means one thing: You've arrived in Hockeytown.

Name the top three
Detroit sports
moments from the second half
of the 20th century.

DREW | **No. 1:** Denny McLain took the mound on September 14, 1968, looking for his 30th victory of the season. As an eight-year-old, I didn't fully appreciate the magnitude of the afternoon. My father took my brother, Brian, and me to what was probably our 10th game that season. It was fun simply watching this incredible team run through the season pretty much unchallenged. I remember my father telling me later that I would understand the historical significance of that day when I got much older. And he was right. I witnessed something that will probably never happen again— a major league pitcher winning 30 games in one season. That's why that moment has no parallel.

No. 2: When Michigan hired Bo Schembechler as its football coach in 1968, he made his objectives quite clear. It was all about beating Ohio State—immediately. The Wolverines stunned the No. 1-ranked Buckeyes in Ann Arbor on November 22, 1969, in Schembechler's first encounter with his old mentor, Ohio State coach Woody Hayes. And a football dynasty took root. The final score, 24-12, remains etched in my brain. I decided on that very day that I would attend the University of Michigan because of that game. And I was only nine. Immediately after the game, I remember taking a bunch of masking tape to an old red football helmet, trying to replicate that peculiar Michigan helmet design I had just noticed for the first time. Bo used a moment to build an era, explaining why that first Ohio State game rates this high.

No. 3: The Tigers became the first team to ever recover from a 3-1 World Series deficit to win the world championship on the road when they defeated the St. Louis Cardinals 4-1 in Game 7 at Busch Stadium on October 10, 1968. The win triggered a spontaneous celebration through city streets that nearly 15 months earlier smoldered from the racial heat of the worst riots in American history at that time. But the 1968 Tigers aren't the only team now to have recovered from a 3-1 deficit. The Kansas City Royals enjoyed a similar resurrection in 1985, thus, dropping the significance of the Tigers' achievement in my mind.

TERRY **No. 1:** The Tigers won the 1968 World Series and united a city. I sat in the right field stands the night the Tigers clinched the pennant against the New York Yankees behind the pitching of wild Joe Sparma. I jumped up and down and screamed like a typical nine-year-old. As we drove through the city that night in celebration, we beeped our car horns in unison with thousands of other happy fans.

But I saw something foreign to me: A black man hugged a white man, and they shook hands.

Drew, how could you grow up in Detroit and not make this your biggest moment? This was one of the few times our city was united.

Much of Detroit had burned to the ground during the summer of 1967 as riots gutted the city. The stench of burning tar and the sound of helicopters hovering, their lights shining on our roofs, remain with me today.

The anger between blacks and whites lingered a year later. But men like Al Kaline, Willie Horton, Denny McLain, Gates Brown, Mickey Stanley, and Earl Wilson helped us forget.

No. 2: We have lift off!

The Captain lifts the Cup. We all raised the Stanley Cup along with captain Steve Yzerman moments after the Red Wings swept the Philadelphia Flyers in the 1997 Stanley Cup finals.

Does the Bad Boys' championship win make the cut?

After 42 years of frustration Lord Stanley's Cup returned to Hockeytown when the Russian Five, Yzerman, Nicklas Lidstrom, and the gang skated circles around the entire league.

We forgot the Darkness with Harkness era. We forgot the bitter sweep to the New Jersey Devils two years earlier when the Wings were pounded into retreat.

Now the Captain held the cup and everybody's heart raced a little faster. People celebrated Yzerman's every accomplishment and cried following every failure. When Yzerman skated around the Joe Louis Arena rink with the Cup raised high, it was as if the entire city was taking this miracle ride with him.

No offense, Drew, but this meant far more to Detroit than Bo and Woody.

No. 3: The Bad Boy Pistons won their first NBA title in 1989.

As Isiah Thomas rubbed the Larry O'Brien championship trophy with champagne on his hands, tears rolled down his cheeks. Pound for pound, Thomas was the toughest player in the NBA. And here he was crying like a baby after the Pistons won the first title in franchise history by sweeping the Los Angeles Lakers in the NBA Finals.

The tears washed away bitter memories of Larry Bird stealing a Thomas pass in the 1987 Eastern Conference Finals and feeding Dennis Johnson for a layup that snatched away certain Pistons victory in Game 5 and led to a Boston Celtics win.

They washed away the pain of losing to the Lakers in the 1988 NBA Finals when Thomas played with a bum ankle and Bill Laimbeer was called for a phantom foul while guarding Kareem Abdul-Jabbar.

They were tears of joy because the Pistons won a title many said they'd never get close to.

 **Name the three best trades in Detroit sports.**

No. 1: The Tigers traded Denny McLain, third baseman Don Wert, and outfielder Elliot Maddox to the Washington Senators for pitcher Joe Coleman, shortstop Eddie Brinkman, and third baseman Aurelio Rodriguez.

This was huge because it constituted grand larceny.

The Tigers wouldn't have won the 1972 American League East Division championship if they hadn't consummated this trade on October 9, 1970. Brinkman and Rodriguez anchored the left side of the Tigers' infield, and Coleman won 20-plus games in 1971 and 1973.

They got rid of somebody who had become a colossal pain in the back pocket. The Tigers had to move McLain after his suspension during part of the 1970 season for associating with known gamblers. McLain's pitching arm was already dead after averaging more than 320 innings pitched in the previous four years and seemingly just as many cortisone injections to reduce inflammation in that right arm.

But the Senators needed a big name to hopefully revive flagging attendance in the nation's capital. It didn't help them. McLain went 10-22 in 1971 before his arm finally gave out. The Senators left the nation's capital after that season, becoming the Texas Rangers in 1972. And many in D.C. believed the lopsided nature of this deal moved fan resentment to the point where the Senators had no other choice but to leave.

No. 2: The Pistons traded forward Adrian Dantley and their 1991 first-round draft pick to the Dallas Mavericks for Mark Aguirre on February 15, 1989. The Pistons had the second-best record in the NBA at the time of the trade, trailing only Cleveland. And they were only a minute away from winning the 1988 NBA championship with Dantley. But coach Chuck Daly and Isiah Thomas decided during a conversation on a plane ride back from Boston a month earlier that they had to make a move. The offense grew too stagnant with Dantley on the floor.

Making this trade when they did required stones the size of coconuts. Why risk breaking something that seemingly was rolling along fine? But great trades demand great risk. Had the Pistons not even reached the NBA Finals after making such a controversial deal, Thomas would have been branded as a selfish boat rocker who had allowed his personal animosity toward Dantley to cloud his judgment.

After Aguirre joined the team in Sacramento, he met privately with Thomas, Bill Laimbeer, and Rick Mahorn. Permit me to paraphrase here. Thomas suggested to his childhood friend that he not screw up.

> "Making [the Dantley-Aguirre trade] when they did required stones the size of coconuts."

He didn't. Aguirre contributed offensively off the bench, helping the Pistons win the back-to-back NBA championships in 1989 and 1990.

No. 3: The Red Wings believed a rugged power forward with a deadly shot was the last missing piece in their hunt for their first Stanley Cup in 42 years. They acquired Brendan Shanahan from the Hartford Whalers for center Keith Primeau and defenseman Paul

Coffey on October 9, 1996. Coffey was a future Hall of Famer, but Detroit coach Scotty Bowman thought he was too careless with the puck in his own zone—a no-no late in the playoffs. This was the biggest trade in Wings history.

TERRY | **No. 1:** The Pistons traded Grant Hill to Orlando for Ben Wallace and Chucky Atkins. This trade put the pieces in place for the 2004 NBA title. Ben Wallace is one of the best off-the-ball defenders in the league, and Atkins helped bring Rasheed Wallace to town—the final piece to the championship puzzle— through a future trade. Hill lacked faith in the Pistons' front office even though Joe Dumars was taking over as team president. Hill was a free agent with a bum foot that would require several surgeries. The Orlando Magic wanted to sign him and pair Hill with budding superstar Tracy McGrady, who would serve as the fluid scorer while Hill would drive the ball to the hole, rebound, and pass to open teammates. But instead of signing with the Magic, Hill helped orchestrate a "sign and trade." He agreed in part due to guilt and in part because he could earn more money. Hill has yet to play a full season with the Magic due to assorted injuries.

No. 2 : The Pistons traded for Rasheed Wallace and Mike James from Atlanta and Boston in a complicated three-way trade that also included draft picks and cash and for what seemed like half of the Pistons roster. Chucky Atkins and Lindsey Hunter went to the Celtics while the Pistons' Bobby Sura and Zeliko Rebraca along with Chris Mills from Boston went to Atlanta. They needed one piece in 2004 to win their first NBA title since 1990. That piece came in a loud-talking, technical-foul-getting guy with a bad reputation and a versatile game.

Wallace joined the Pistons and immediately made them the best starting five in the NBA. He did not need to play a major role but his defense, rebounding, and deadly jump shot put the Pistons on top.

No. 3: The Tigers traded for Ty Cobb, who owned 90 hitting records by the time he retired from Detroit after 22 years. Few know that Cobb was obtained via trade from the Class C South Atlantic (Salley) League. The Tigers gave up pitcher Eddie Cicotte, and paid Augusta $700 and an additional $50 for "immediate delivery." Cobb immediately went to work during his rookie season in 1905. A few weeks after his mother, Amanda, shot his father, W.H., he was in the Tigers lineup, beginning a long stormy run that was mixed with controversy and spectacular hitting. Some view Cobb the greatest hitter of the century.

# Name the three worst trades in Detroit sports.

DREW | **No. 1:** The Pistons traded Dave DeBusschere to the New York Knicks for center Walt Bellamy and guard Howie Komives on December 19, 1968. This trade was so reviled in my neighborhood when I was a kid that whenever anybody got suckered in a trade of baseball cards, we always said he got "Komived." Whenever your name assumes the verb form, you know you're in trouble. DeBusschere was a Detroit star in high school at Austin High, in college at the University of Detroit, and professionally as a Pistons player and eventually coach. Despite the popularity of Dave Bing, I sincerely believe the Pistons lost a lot of fan support when they shipped out DeBusschere. And it killed everyone in the city watching DeBusschere's contributions lead the Knicks to their first NBA championship two years later in 1970.

"[The DeBusschere] trade was so reviled in my neighborhood when I was a kid that whenever anybody got suckered in a trade of baseball cards, we always said he got 'Komived.'"

No. 2: Who knew?

Who would have believed that the Lions' decision to trade quarterback Bobby Layne to the Pittsburgh Steelers midway through the 1958 season would have triggered a four-decade drought of competent quarterbacking. It seemed innocent enough at the time. Layne had a proclivity for pushing the limits with his partying. If there was a 1 p.m. kickoff, he'd get to the stadium by 12:55 p.m., liberate his system of the toxins from the previous evening, and play one helluva game. But the Lions had enough of his antics, and they were pretty confident in his replacement, Tobin Rote, who had replaced an injured Layne late in the 1957 season. Rote quarterbacked the Lions to their last NFL championship in 1957. The Lions have only won a single playoff game since that 1957 championship game, and just as long-suffering Boston Red Sox fans had their "Curse of the Bambino" because they sold Babe Ruth to the New York Yankees, some Lions fans believe the organization's stubbornness with their fearless leader created a blight that remains to this day.

No. 3: Desperate to excite their fans with the opening of Comerica Park in 2000, the Tigers traded for slugging outfielder Juan Gonzalez, acquiring him and reliever Danny Patterson from the Texas Rangers on November 2, 1999, for pitcher Justin Thompson, outfielder Gabe Kapler, infielder Frank Catalanatto, and minor league closer Francisco Cordero.

This ranks as one of the worst trades because it was one of the worst insults to fan intelligence. Here the Tigers were constructing a ballpark with sizeable dimensions in the left and center field. So what do you do? You trade your best left-handed pitcher for a right-handed power hitter. Tigers owner Mike Ilitch and his general manager, Randy Smith, confused desperation with daring.

Gonzalez was one of the game's preeminent run producers during that era, averaging 140 RBI in the previous four seasons. But he had one more year remaining on his contract, and the Rangers weren't willing to commit big money to somebody with recurring back problems. They were looking for a sucker, and the Tigers obliged.

Gonzalez drove in only 67 runs in his one year in Detroit.

The Rangers were once the Washington Senators in a former life. So perhaps this was their revenge for the Denny McLain debacle nearly 20 years earlier.

TERRY | **No. 1:** The Lions traded their 1993 first-round draft pick, the eighth selection overall, to the New Orleans Saints for linebacker Pat Swilling. This was the worst trade ever in Detroit because it was one of the most confusing. The Lions needed a pass rusher, and Swilling was one of the best, although word out of New Orleans was he was on the decline. So why turn him into a cover linebacker? I can't tell you the number of times Swilling shouted, "Pat Swilling don't do pass coverage." And, of course, adding insult to injury was that the Saints drafted offensive tackle Willie Roaf, who turned out to be one of the best linemen of his era. And what was the Lions' weakness during the Barry Sanders era?

The offensive line.

Swilling turned Lions fans off before his first trip to town. Before signing a contract with the team, he demanded that the team bring Joe Schmidt's number 56 out of retirement so he could wear it. In two seasons, Swilling recorded just 10 sacks and three interceptions before being traded to Oakland.

No. 2: The Tigers traded prime pitching prospect John Smoltz to the Atlanta Braves for veteran pitcher Doyle Alexander. On the short term this was a great trade. Alexander went 9-0 with a 1.53 earned run average propelling the Tigers to the 1987 division title. But they were upset by Minnesota in the division series, and Alexander was 34-39 the final three years of his career in Detroit.

Meanwhile, Smoltz is 177-128 during his 17 seasons with the Braves and has been part of one of the greatest pitching staffs in baseball history. He finished 24-8 in 1996 and was 17-3 two seasons later. Tigers fans cringe every time he takes the mound.

No. 3: The Pistons acquired center William Bedford from Phoenix in 1988 for a 1998 first-round draft choice. Pistons general manager Jack McCloskey loved Bedford's potential. He was a seven-footer who could handle the ball and shoot the rock, but he never put his potential to good use. Bedford had drug and sexual addictions that prevented him from focusing on the game of basketball.

I once chided him for shooting balls from out of bounds during warmups rather than working on his inside moves.

"You never know when we might need a four-point shot," he said.

He always reminded me of a child who had grown into a large man's body that he did not know how to handle.

Here is all you need to know about Bedford. Remember that time in L.A., Drew, when you and I were driving with him on the Santa Monica Freeway? He was leaning out of the car trying to get a woman's phone number.

 **If the United States Senate possessed the power to impeach one person in Detroit sports, who would that be?**

DREW Tigers owner Walter O. Briggs was a morally vacuous figure, vowing to never have a black ballplayer on his team. Such thinking was deplorable, but especially in Detroit where the growing strength of the automobile industry through the first half of the 20th century was reflected in the migration of Southern blacks northward to man the assembly lines.

Detroit symbolized opportunity for all, but Briggs's racial stubbornness attached a stigma to the Tigers organization that remained long after the Tigers signed their first black player, catcher Ozzie Virgil, in 1958. The Tigers were the next-to-last major league team to break the color barrier. The Boston Red Sox pulled up the rear, finally signing their first black player in 1959.

No evidence has ever surfaced stating that blacks were denied access into Briggs Stadium during the 24 years of Briggs's ownership. But as the black population in Detroit grew during the post–World War II boom, there was a growing sense that they weren't welcomed at the stadium, a slight that was passed down through generations.

Briggs's legacy as the Tigers owner was story after story shared in families like my own where elders told impressionable youngsters that the Tigers weren't worth supporting because they didn't like black people. Briggs's bigotry did more to disparage Detroit's image than any prominent sports figure.

The problem was that the perception of exclusion remained after Briggs sold the team to Kalamazoo broadcasting magnate John Fetzer in 1962. It was a big deal in my house whenever the Tigers had two blacks in the starting lineup—and that was in the late 1960s and early 1970s. Sports teams not only have a competitive obligation to their fans, but they're also obliged to share a sense of community. Briggs let down this city with his archaic thinking, and for those actions, he should have any association with Detroit stripped away.

TERRY | Let's be clear about this. I, in no way, want Lions owner Bill Ford Sr. impeached from our community. I simply wish someone else had owned the Lions the past half decade.

The man is too kind. He allows people to stick around too long to do their jobs. That is why the Russ Thomas era lasted too long. That is why the Chuck Schmidt era lasted too long. And his patience and kindness is why I fear the Matt Millen era will last too long.

The Lions need a tough and angry SOB to own this team. They need someone to hold incompetent people accountable and issue the one-way bus tickets out of town that former coach Bobby Ross used to talk about.

Here is all you need to know about Lions football. They've won one playoff game since winning the 1957 NFL championship game. They've never been to a Super Bowl, and they are 312-389-17 since 1957.

So how did Ford fix this? He hired Millen out of the broadcast booth, a guy with no front-office experience. He hired Millen because his son, Bill Ford Jr., liked talking to him before games. And because Millen talked a good game, the Lions figured he'd win games for them.

But things got worse. The Lions are 21-59 since Chicago Bears kicker Paul Edinger hit that field goal that knocked the 2000 team from the playoffs.

Is the long suffering of the Lions enough of a crime to impeach Bill Ford Sr.?

Millen has been a disaster. But who put him in place? And who gave him a contract extension? It was Bill Ford Sr.

Former Lions coach Wayne Fontes used to shower "Mr. Ford" with praise calling him "the cream of the crop. The best owner in the NFL." That's because Fontes knew if he softened up the owner he could stick around a few more years and cement himself as both the winningest and losingest coach in Lions history.

It breaks my heart to write this because Ford Sr. is a hell of a guy. He does plenty of charity work and is one of the leaders of our community. Detroit is better because of the Ford family.

When I talk to him, I privately wish him and the team well. I want him to find the magic potion to turn this franchise around. But I do not have much faith it will happen.

# Who was the most overrated player in Detroit sports?

DREW | I can hear you complaining already, Terry. How can you penalize a college kid for being overhyped? How is that fair? Waah-waah-waah.

It's a fine whine heard quite often in Ann Arbor, because when Michigan fans look at the legacy of quarterback Drew Henson, they'll see someone who never came close to reaching the level of expectations.

But, face it, folks—Henson was a bust.

He was projected as a Heisman Trophy winner, the first player taken in the NFL draft, the starting third baseman for the New York Yankees, and the second coming of Roger Staubach with the Dallas Cowboys.

Instead, he serves as a monument to unrealized potential.

In three years at Michigan, he had one shining moment—engineering a victory at Ohio State that gave the Wolverines a share of the Big Ten championship in 2000 during his junior season.

A hot baseball prospect, Henson stunned Michigan fans the following winter when he signed a six-year, $17 million contract with the Yankees. The plan called for no more than two years of seasoning in the minor leagues and then elevation to the parent club where he would man the left side of the Yankees infield with Derek Jeter.

But there was a little problem. Henson couldn't hit a minor league curveball.

Drew Henson was a good quarterback at Michigan but was he a victim of hype or a casualty of big money?

The Yankees bought out Henson's contract following the 2003 season, and he returned to football. Many believed that was his better vocation anyway. Twenty teams watched Henson work out in early 2004. He signed an eight-year deal with the Cowboys, and "America's Team" thought it found its newest savior.

But there was a little problem. Henson couldn't handle the speed of the pro game.

Following the 2005 season, Henson, relegated to No. 3 on the Cowboys' quarterback depth chart, signed on to play in NFL Europe in the spring of 2006 in a last-ditch effort to resuscitate his professional career.

The talent was always there, but now you wonder if there isn't an equal portion of tenacity. Henson's biggest crime was that he believed the hype.

Michigan has enjoyed its share of football stars during its 125-plus-year history, but it never had a more heavily promoted recruit than the six-foot-four quarterback who many targeted as the finest player to ever wear the Maize and Blue—and that was while he was still a senior at Brighton (Michigan) High School.

Henson committed to Michigan coach Lloyd Carr as a high school sophomore, but he insisted on an important stipulation. If Henson committed early, Carr couldn't sign another quarterback—a decision that hurt the Michigan program after Henson bolted following three years because it didn't have a suitable replacement ready.

Carr learned his lesson, telling me in 2001 that he'll never again make such a deal with a recruit.

TERRY | I don't know who passed out the memo. But we were all told that former Tiger Bobby Higginson was a franchise player.

And we bought into it. And believed it even when he kept putting up mediocre numbers.

From 1995 to 2004, the Tigers were Higginson's team. He sat in the big locker right by the entrance, and when the media needed a read on the state of the Tigers, they turned to Higginson. He played the role of team spokesperson well, although many said he opened his mouth too much.

"Higgy" was paid like a superstar, but did not play like one. He earned $11,850,000 in 2003 and batted .235 with 14 home runs and 52 RBI. Higginson batted .272 for his career, and the Tigers never had a winning season with him even though they paid him more than $52 million during a 10-year career.

His hype was so large that even the New York Yankees considered trading for him, but Tigers owner Mike Ilitch loved Higginson and felt he had to do whatever he could to keep him.

That might have been Ilitch's biggest screw-up.

Instead Higginson became the poster boy of what went wrong with the Tigers. When you think of the team's decade of losing, you think of Higginson because he was there for most of the free fall and he never lived up to expectations.

Drew, you are wrong about Henson. He is not overrated. The dude was a very good quarterback at Michigan. He simply got blinded by George Steinbrenner's money. If he had ignored baseball and focused on football, he would have been a star in the NFL.

The media and fans fell for Higginson because he hustled and played hard, often playing over pain. That is why many of us rooted for him. He was arrogant at times, but we always fall for those who try hard. I would never accuse Higginson of not trying. He just was not good enough for what the Tigers needed.

In the final analysis he was a marginal player on a very bad team who was paid as though he was the Most Valuable Player of a championship team.

Name Detroit's top three all-time sports characters.

TERRY

No. 1: Dennis Rodman was a kid even at age 30. He loved to play video games, cruise the mall, drink milkshakes, and hang with kids nearly half his age. A 17-year-old friend of Rodman once told me he stopped hanging with "The Worm" because he was too immature.

Rodman, who was a fan favorite, loved to pump his fist to fire up the Pistons crowd, and he cried every time he won a big award.

He became the king of tattoos, dated Madonna, and gave everybody a scare in 1994 when he was in his truck outside The Palace with a loaded gun.

No. 2: Darryl Dawkins was only a Piston for short periods of the 1988 and 1989 seasons, but how can you not include someone nicknamed "Chocolate Thunder from the Planet Lovetron"?

By the time he landed in Detroit, his career was in full decline, but his sense of humor was better than ever. During a practice session in Sacramento, he grabbed a black 33-gallon garbage bag, frowning as he flipped the bag over and over.

Finally, he said, "Look. It's Rick Mahorn's momma's underwear."

The whole team broke up in laughter, including Mahorn.

But there was a sensitive side to Dawkins, too. When Jack McCloskey cut him from the team in 1989, the big guy cried.

No. 3: Jose Lima was the loudest and funniest guy in the Tigers clubhouse. He had a wild streak, too. Lima often came to the park with different hair colors and strange hairdos. And he was always singing—well, trying to sing. Lima Time was always Fun Time.

But the fun didn't last because he pitched terribly while in Detroit. Lima was 17–32 during his two Tigers tours here. He had earned run averages of 6.11, 5.70, 4.71, and 7.77 before being shipped out of town for the last time.

But "Lima Time" sure was a wonderful time. That is until he actually pitched.

DREW | **No. 1:** Wayne Fontes, the Lions head coach from 1988 to 1996, became a cartoon, and he didn't care that everybody laughed. Fontes figured he got the last laugh, winning more games (67) than any other head coach in Lions history. But Fontes also lost more games (71) than any coach in franchise history. He's the face of the Lions, complete with the Mickey Mouse ears he wore during a press conference to call attention to one of his charities supporting children. Head coaches should command respect. Fontes drew chuckles.

No. 2: As the Tigers manager from 1979 to 1994, Sparky Anderson's grammatically challenged whimsy proved disarmingly effective with his players and media. He didn't run away from his modest education. "Ain't nobody here building rockets," he once told me in his office. He kept things simple, and that's the best way to find success in baseball.

No. 3: Mark Fidrych, a Tigers pitcher from 1976 to 1980, was a baseball whisperer, believing that he had special communicative powers with the horsehide. There was no word on whether the baseball ever talked back to Fidrych. He wouldn't use baseballs that he believed were uncooperative. But when you win 19 games as he did during his rookie season in 1976, you're forgiven as an eccentric.

 Who is the biggest opposing villain in Detroit sports history?

DREW C'mon Terry, how can a man have his face occupy every square of a roll of toilet paper and not be the biggest villain?

It's Wayne Woodrow Hayes, my friend, or as he was commonly called during my time as a student at the University of Michigan—that @#$%&#@& Woody.

One of my college roommate's most prized possessions was a roll of toilet paper with the image of a maniacal senior citizen wearing that ever-present baseball cap with the block O. The idea of the product was that Michigan fans could happily and literally rub Hayes's nose in it at our convenience.

But my roommate never used the paper. He kept it on display. The message was that he despised Woody Hayes so much that he would even consider soiling Hayes's face in the name of hygiene.

Hayes was a loathsome figure because he joyously spat on anything associated with the state of Michigan. That was his plan when he first arrived in Columbus in 1950. The Buckeyes were the Wolverines' personal whipping post, and Hayes changed the mindset of the rivalry. He injected animosity. He felt there was nothing wrong with Ohioans openly expressing their disgust to "that school up north" as he called it. He never referred to Michigan by name. That would place the Wolverines on an equal plane with the Buckeyes.

It was mad genius.

Ohio State had the nation's No. 1-ranked team in 1968, and the Wolverines were struggling in the final days of the Bump Elliott coaching administration. Hayes didn't call off the dogs, driving for a late touchdown and giving the Buckeyes a 48-14 lead. But then Hayes went for a two-point conversion. Ohio State scored and won 50-14. It was classless. It was bush league. It was Hayes at his churlishness worst.

Michigan hired Bo Schembechler, a Hayes protégé at Ohio State, with one purpose. Beat the old man!

Schembechler beat Hayes that first year, stunning the No. 1-ranked Buckeyes in Ann Arbor on November 22, 1969, 24-12 and setting the tone for one of the more emotionally charged battlegrounds in college football. Watching Hayes suffer on the sidelines was more enjoyable than the Michigan victory itself. Remember the sight of him kicking the yard marker in disgust after an Ohio State turnover in the 1971 game in Ann Arbor?

The Schembechler–Hayes battle wouldn't have worked here without the adversarial element that Hayes provided.

TERRY | Hey, baby boy, some of us don't care about Michigan football. Half the state would have welcomed Woody Hayes if he were coming to coach at Michigan State.

Former Colorado Avs forward Claude Lemieux needs a police escort every time he travels to Michigan. He is easily the most hated athlete in our lifetime.

I was in the Avalanche dressing room minutes after Lemieux drilled Red Wings forward Chris Draper into the boards in Game 6 of the 1996 Western Conference Finals. The villain lay on a training table answering questions about the hit. He showed no remorse and did not care about Draper's health. He brushed aside questions about Draper and said he was happy with the results.

Draper required 30 stitches in the face, and his jaw was wired shut for 16 days.

Lemieux always got under a player's skin. He scored big playoff goals for the New Jersey Devils and Avalanche, and he was like the bad wrestler in the WWE fans came to boo. He resorted to illegal tactics, and his hit of Draper was the last straw.

If the Wings were not going to pay Lemieux back, the fans would.

That is why March 26, 1997, is one of the most famous days in Wings history. That was when the Wings' Darren McCarty got revenge by beating the snot out of Turtle Lemieux at Joe Louis Arena.

It brought glee to Wings fans, and Lemieux the coward got what he deserved. Wings fans were behind every punch "D Mac" threw.

We are a forgiving city.

People forgave Michael Jordan for calling the Bad Boys Pistons bad champions. They even welcomed Chris Chelios from Chicago where he was a bad man who agitated the Wings. They even viewed Hayes as a tragic figure at the end.

But Detroit fans will always hate Lemieux no matter what direction his life turns.

If you drive by Joe Louis Arena, you can still hear people cheering the Lemieux beating.

 **Name Detroit's top three good guys in sports.**

No. 1: Why shouldn't simple elegance and proper
D R E W   decorum typify the ultimate "good guy"? There's no
question that former Michigan State star Steve Smith, a man who
contributed millions to his university for an academic center that
honored his mother, should top this list. The Clara Bell Smith
Academic Center is Smith's most enduring legacy. I saw Smith in
October 2005 during the Michigan–Michigan State game in East
Lansing. It was the day after he retired from the NBA following a 14-
year career that produced a world championship in 2003, an NBA All-
Star Game appearance in 1998, and an Olympic gold medal in 2000.
And I congratulated him on being a gentleman. I told him that he was
the classiest athlete Detroit sports had ever seen. Smith beamed in
appreciation at the acknowledgment. It meant a lot to him that
someone didn't praise him for his philanthropy or his 13,000-plus
points in the NBA, but rather simply for his being a good, decent
individual.

No. 2: When Willie Horton, a Tigers outfielder from 1963 to 1977
who was raised in northwest Detroit, heard of his hometown going up
in flames during the early stages of the 1967 riots, he put on his Tigers
uniform and went into the affected neighborhoods. He believed that if
the rioters and looters saw him, they would stop. It was naïve thinking.
But it also was evidence of somebody who cared deeply about his

hometown and wouldn't just stand idle during Detroit's worst crisis—
and that's worthy of recognition in my book.

No. 3:   Tom Izzo—Michigan State's basketball coach (1994-
present)—pulled me aside after the Spartans stunned Kentucky in 1999
to earn the Spartans' first visit to the Final Four in 20 years. Izzo was a
new national star, but he told me to never let him forget that he was
still "nothing more than a little (expletive) from the [Upper
Pennisula]." He might currently be the single most recognizable sports
figure in the state of Michigan. The man is big time, but he's
determined to stay grounded. The fact that he doesn't forget from
where he came merits acknowledgment on my list.

T E R R Y | **No. 1:**   I see we both agreed that Steve Smith is the
No. 1 good guy. We both have had great dealings with
him, and there is no better choice. Smith, the skinny kid from Detroit
Pershing High School, enjoyed a fine college career at Michigan State
and several NBA teams. He even earned a world championship ring
with San Antonio. But Smitty cared about people. In 1997, he donated
$2.5 million to build the $7.5 million Clara Bell Smith Student-
Athlete Academic Center at Michigan State University. It was the
largest contribution ever from a professional athlete. The facility was
named after Smith's mother, who died of cancer in 1992. He also
contributed to the Steve Smith Scholarship Fund for students at
Pershing.

He also had time for everybody. I remember telling Smith about
building a new home. I knew he had talked to his dad about it, because
the next time I saw Smith, he was relaying tips from his father.

"And he said if you build a walk-out basement, make sure you get
a heavy duty sink so you can wash your hands after yardwork," Smith
told me.

How many athletes give you housing tips?

No. 2:   A star at Detroit Catholic Central, Frank Tanana threw hard
and lived hard through the first chapter of his baseball career. He won

93 games with the California Angels in the first eight years of his career. But he lost the speed on his fastball and developed arm problems. Still, he gained perspective on his life. He found Jesus Christ after surgery to repair his left pitching arm. He formed prayer groups, disciplined teammates, and taught men how to study the scriptures. Tanana treated everybody with respect. He returned home and pitched for the Tigers (1985-1992), the highlight of which was pitching a shutout in a 1-0 victory against Toronto on the last day of the 1987 regular season, earning the Tigers their last division championship.

No. 3: Being a good guy merely means taking the time to converse with a two-year-old. Martin Lapointe, one of the more popular Red Wings players, frequented a Southfield coffee shop that my then-two-year-old daughter, Celine, and I went to every morning before delivering her to her babysitter. One morning, I introduced Lapointe to Celine. Athletes meet people all of the time, so you never really expect them to be anything more than cordial. But when Celine and I ran into Lapointe again a few weeks later, he watched with great interest as Celine showed him a decorative sticker plastered on her arm. And customers were charmed at the sight of an athlete taking a minute to engage in the antics of a child. My daughter never forgot those conversations. She still asks how the "hockey man" is doing in his new city. (Lapointe signed with Boston as a free agent in 2001 after spending the first 10 years of his career in Detroit.)

Q It's generally agreed that the first three faces of granite on Detroit's Mount Rushmore are Joe Louis, Gordie Howe, and Isiah Thomas. But who deserves the fourth spot—Al Kaline or Ty Cobb?

DREW Defending Cobb is comparable to praising a bank robber for the creativity of the getaway. The man was a racist, a jerk, (insert whatever derogatory descriptions of your choosing here). But in this argument, you must distinguish the athlete from the ass. Cobb's 4,191 career base hits stood as the major league standard for nearly 60 years, and 3,900 of those hits came during his 21 years in Detroit. Cobb received seven more votes than the immortal Babe Ruth in the first Baseball Hall of Fame induction vote in 1936. You can't ignore that, regardless of the man's moral flaws. If he weren't the poster child for Ku Klux Klan recruiting, this would have been a no-brainer, especially when you factor in the class and dignity of Kaline's career in Detroit.

But this is a debate about those Detroit athletes who were unique to their respective sports. Mount Rushmore is reserved for those with no peers. You can make the argument that Louis and Howe are still regarded today as the very best who ever participated in their particular sports. And Isiah belongs for disproving the popularly held conviction that you can't build NBA championships around the little guy.

Under those parameters, Kaline doesn't come close.

Cobb hated anybody who was different from him. He despised blacks, Jews, Catholics, and Northerners. He reportedly got into a scuffle with a black groundskeeper at a ballpark in Augusta, Georgia, and supposedly choked the man's wife when she tried intervening in the dispute. And long, long, long before Ron Artest crossed the line and went into stands after fans, Cobb charged into the stands in New York, seeking retaliation against a heckler. When he got into the crowd, Cobb realized that the man had only one hand because of workplace accident. It didn't matter to Cobb. He still beat the poor man into submission and was subsequently suspended from the game.

But such conduct still can't diminish the following résumé:

He led the American League in hits and slugging percentage eight times, stolen bases six times, runs scored five times, runs batted in four times, doubles three times, and home runs once. And he batted .400 for a season three times.

He wasn't a good citizen. But I wouldn't necessarily want a Boy Scout in my lineup if I wanted to win.

TERRY Now I see why they call you evil, Drew. You wanted Ty Cobb on the Mount Rushmore of Detroit sports ahead of Al Kaline?

Who's next?

Jack the Ripper? Claude Lemieux?

There is no question Cobb was a great ballplayer and deserves a spot in the Baseball Hall of Fame. But his violent and racist ways should not grant him such an honor.

Kaline embodied greatness and goodness at the same time. Kaline is Mr. Tiger and remains a great ambassador for the ball club as a consultant. The next harsh word you hear about Kaline will be the first one. Here is how big Kaline was to me as a kid growing up on Detroit's west side.

I needed batteries for my transistor radio. So I walked to the hardware store to buy them. When I carried them up to the counter to pay for them, I noticed the words *alkaline batteries* printed along the side.

I thought, "Wow, Al Kaline is so great that he has batteries named after him!"

And here is how important he was to the team. A Tigers manager made one of the biggest gambles in sports history just to get Kaline into the lineup for the 1968 World Series, inserting Mickey Stanley at shortstop to get a returning Kaline (broken wrist) into the lineup.

No one dug into the right field corner like Kaline. It was as if he knew every crack and every twist on that wall. He knew where it was going to bounce, and he had a strong arm to whiz it quickly into the infield. He became the youngest batting champion (hitting .340 with 27 home runs) in baseball history in 1955 at the tender age of 20, and he and Cobb are the only Tigers to register 3,000 hits. The only annoying thing about Kaline is his 399 home runs.

Can we get a recount to see if he actually hit 400?

Or maybe he can come back and hit one more?

Every kid grew up wanting to be Kaline. He played the game the way it was supposed to be played, and he played with great class, dignity, and grace.

And I don't say this just because he is a good guy. Kaline made 15 All-Star teams and won 11 Gold Gloves. He was elected to Baseball's Hall of Fame in 1980 on the first ballot, the same year the Tigers retired his No. 6.

Who was the most underrated superstar in Detroit sports?

DREW | Mickey Lolich happily lived under the radar. It didn't bother him that Denny McLain warranted all of the acclaim during the Tigers' magical 1968 season, just so long as opponents knew that he was equally as talented a big-game pitcher as McLain.

And they knew it.

St. Louis Cardinals catcher Tim McCarver recalled the days leading up to the 1968 World Series between his National League champion Cards and the AL pennant-waving Tigers. In an HBO documentary on the 1968 Tigers, McCarver said that teammate Roger Maris warned his confident teammates that the left-handed Lolich was the guy they should worry about most.

They could handle McLain, who had become the first 30-game winner in more than 30 years. But the Cardinals believed Lolich's repertoire was more overpowering.

Lolich was the Most Valuable Player of the 1968 World Series, winning three games, including the Tigers' 4-1 Series-clinching victory in Game 7 in St. Louis.

That achievement still didn't get Lolich the headlines he deserved. He didn't exactly look the part of a media "cover boy." Was the man born fat? The jowly face and the protruding gut were features reminiscent of the guy next door who's the big gun on his beer league softball team.

Was Mickey Lolich the top man who flew under Detroit's radar?

But that's exactly what made Lolich more embraceable to the common fan. He looked just like us. OK, he probably should have eaten more vegetables than donuts. But he never feared the challenge and he got the job done. Lolich became the Tigers' No. 1 starter in 1970 after McLain's suspension for associating with gamblers.

Lolich led the majors in victories (25) in 1971, and from 1971 to 1973 only the Chicago White Sox's Wilbur Wood won more games than Lolich in the American League. But Lolich never won a Cy Young Award, given to the league's top pitcher in a season. But it wasn't a slight worn as a grudge. When Lolich retired from baseball in 1978, he happily accepted his legacy as a power pitcher who was never more powerful than when his teammates needed it most that October in 1968.

It didn't matter that few outside of Detroit recognized him. He opened a donut shop (it figures, doesn't it?) in Lake Orion, Michigan, and was known to share his baseball memories with customers.

TERRY | Here is what people know about former Piston Rick Mahorn. He was tough and nasty, and didn't score a lot of points. He knocked people down and did not help them up.

Here is what they don't know. He was the backbone of the Pistons' championship runs. If you are going to call yourselves Bad Boys, you need an enforcer to back up your words. That is what Mahorn did. And he did it well.

Mahorn averaged 6.9 points and 6.2 rebounds a year. Those are not Hall of Fame numbers, but he lasted 18 years in the NBA because he provided another set of values. When the Pistons won their first title in 1989, they left Mahorn off the expansion protected list, thinking no one would select him because of his advanced age and back problems.

But the Minnesota Timberwolves picked him because of intangibles that do not show up in stat sheets. He was a leader who the Timberwolves believed would show their young players the path to professionalism.

He could have done that if he actually had reported. But Mahorn loved the Pistons so much he did not want to play anywhere else. He forced the Wolves to trade him.

Even though the Pistons won another title after Mahorn left, it signaled the beginning of the end of this team. They were not as tough in the paint and they were not as versatile defensively. Although Mahorn stood six feet, 10 inches and is regarded as a plodder, he used to guard James Worthy of the Los Angeles Lakers, who happens to be one of the most athletic small forwards in NBA history.

Mahorn calmed things down when they got out of hand. He taught Bill Laimbeer how to be a tougher player, and when Isiah Thomas needed a helping hand, Mahorn was there to give it to him.

We hear a lot about Joe Dumars, Vinnie Johnson, John Salley, Dennis Rodman, Laimbeer, and Thomas. They were great players who deserve every piece of credit they got. But Mahorn was the rock that kept the pieces from falling apart.

# What's the best classic uniform in Detroit sports?

DREW | One of my more vivid memories as a little boy was my father taking me to my first game at Tiger Stadium in 1966. Color TV wasn't the household norm then, so the green of the grass and the old wood-splintered seats provided a dimension I had never experienced.

But what stood out the most was watching Al Kaline trot out to right field in a clean, crisp home uniform. It was blinding.

It was as though extra bleach had been used to clean it, bringing a bold character to the white. The uniform screamed at fans, "I'm a Detroit Tiger!"

To this day, I defy anyone to show me a home white baseball uniform that could seamlessly blend into a winter snowfall.

The Tigers' home look is No. 1 because it symbolizes tradition more than other Detroit sports uniform. It hasn't changed in 100 years. The Old English D stitched across the right breast with the subtle black piping possesses the same cache as the New York Yankees' home pinstripes or the Boston Red Sox's red socks.

Today, it's all about merchandising. If a team isn't selling tens of thousands of its jerseys to teenagers for $100 a pop, it's time to bring in the market researchers to determine what's gone wrong and what changes are needed.

The Tigers' uniform doesn't sell particularly well. According to 2004 numbers from Major League Baseball, the Tigers are in the bottom third of merchandise sold.

But don't hold your breath waiting for the designers at Nike and Reebok to knock on the Tigers' door with suggestions about tinkering with the team's home look. And that alone is cause for popping champagne corks.

There's a simplicity to the Tigers uniform that's refreshing, and since baseball is a sport that directly ties its present and future to its past, the Tigers' look is living history.

Put on the uniform and a player knows it's the same that Ty Cobb wore at the turn of the 20th century and that Hank Greenberg and Charlie Gehringer donned four decades later.

TERRY The day Joe Dumars was named Pistons team president in June 2000, he chatted with writers about his game plan for transforming the franchise. Dumars often grumbled about the teal and white uniform color scheme that the team's previous administration introduced in 1996. And when a reporter asked him that first day if he planned to change the uniform, Dumars gleefully said he was already working on it.

A year later Dumars brought the Pistons back to their championship roots on the floor and in their look.

The red, white, and blue color combination with a basic block-lettered Pistons stitched across the chest is the best sports look in Michigan. It's not pretentious.

This is "The D," and we don't need splash or pastel colors unless we're going clubbing later for a night of dancing. The Pistons' theme is "Going to work," and the teal uniforms didn't work.

Instead, the uniforms were a joke.

Sometimes simple is best. There is nothing that stands out in the new/old Pistons uniform, but it represents this city well because it is

The late 1990s look of the Pistons was more modern than classic. Which uniform in Detroit is never out of style: the Pistons' traditional red, white, and blue look or the Tigers' pinstripes?

something you look cool hanging out with the fellas at the corner bar or while strolling around Eastern Market on a lazy Saturday.

Boodini, I agree with what you said about the simplicity of the Tigers uniform. It is basically the same thing as the Pistons uniform, only with sleeves.

I even love the new red Pistons uniforms that are becoming hot sellers in our community.

Marketing research determined that teal was the hot color in sports uniforms. Merchandising was becoming an important revenue source for the NBA, so the league gave the Pistons the green light, or shall we say the teal light, to alter their look as well as their logo.

Remember the horse's head and the tailpipes? People kept trying to figure out what it meant. It was supposed to symbolize the pumping pistons generating a car engine's horsepower. It was a ridiculous stretch.

The basketball uniform has changed over the last 20 years. The hot pants shorts of the 1980s changed to the baggy shorts of the 1990s and the present. The length of the shorts and the shape of the top might change once again, but, thankfully, Dumars will ensure that the Pistons will always remain loyal to the red, white, and blue.

The lesson in all of this is marketing research does not apply to Detroit. We like it plain and simple.

Who is the most influential woman in Detroit sports?

DREW | Micki King's influence stretched far beyond the boundaries of the Detroit area. She opened doors previously closed to women in sports, taking an instrumental role in the development of Title IX, the federal law that mandated equity between men's and women's intercollegiate athletics.

The Pontiac native won a gold medal in springboard diving at the 1972 Munich Olympics. Earlier that year, President Richard Nixon signed into law Title IX of the Education Amendments. But its language was too broad in scope, making enforcement difficult in its infancy.

King's trailblazing path didn't begin until the following year. King had joined the U.S. Air Force soon after graduating from Michigan in 1966, and she became the first female coach at the then-all male Air Force Academy in 1973. She became the first woman to coach a male

"[Micki King] didn't fear expressing her disgust at how she made less money coaching the men's team than a male coach would have made."

athlete to an NCAA championship in 1974 when one of her divers won the three-meter platform competition.

It was then that King recognized the inequities in coaching salaries between men and women. She didn't fear expressing her disgust at how she made less money coaching the men's team than a male coach would have made. Although the concept of gender equity was the law of the land, change would come grudgingly slow. It wasn't until 1982 when the NCAA finally extended scholarships in women's sports.

It was that year when King retired from the U.S. Air Force after 26 years with the rank of colonel. But that didn't end her involvement in promoting women's sports. She joined the University of Kentucky as assistant athletic director and remains involved with the U.S. Olympic Committee as an adviser.

TERRY | Denise Ilitch is not an athlete. She is no longer part of Ilitch Holdings, which owns the Tigers and Red Wings, or affiliated with any team. But that is temporary.

Trust me. She will play a major role with the Tigers and Red Wings again. Right now she is out of sports working the political scene. She raised more than $1 million to help elect Jennifer Granholm for governor and appears on local television giving her views on important topics and events.

Ilitch is out of the loop now. But when she served as president of Ilitch Holdings, she not only helped decide the products that fueled Ilitch Holdings, but she sat on boards that made decisions about the Tigers and Red Wings.

She sat on the committee that brought Jimmy Devellano in town to run the Red Wings. Currently Ilitch is running a consulting firm that dabbles in the sports world.

A few years ago I wrote a column saying the Tigers wanted to sell the team and build the new Joe Louis Arena behind the Fox Theater. Denise Ilitch did not like the story, and she contacted me.

We hashed out our differences during lunch at the Detroit Athletic Club. It was the first time I realized that she was a power broker and how much influence she had on the sports world.

When the Lions were building Ford Field next to Comerica Park, Denise Ilitch was the toughest and most outspoken person at the negotiating table. She fought hard for her family.

If you don't believe me, ask Lions president Tom Lewand.

The Ilitch family will build more entertainment venues, and Denise Ilitch will have a major say in negotiations.

She will also get her hands back on the Tigers and Red Wings, two of the most important businesses in Detroit.

Name the top three all-time Detroit sports jerks.

TERRY

No. 1: The nickname "Mount St. Morris" fit perfectly for the guy who wore a permanent scowl under a bush mustache. Jack Morris once created a national furor when he told a woman sportswriter for the *Detroit Free Press* that he didn't talk to women unless he was having sex with them. Sometimes asking him questions at his postgame press conferences was comparable to waving a red flag in front of a bull. And most of the time Morris won. From 1979 to 1992 he won more games (223) than any other pitcher in the major leagues. But many believe that his battles with the media remain the primary reason why he hasn't fared well in Hall of Fame voting. The writers and broadcasters whom he gave such a hard time are giving a little something back to him.

No. 2: Even Charley Schmidt, one of the true gentlemen of the game, got into two fistfights with Ty Cobb. Once he battled Cobb for slapping a black woman. Cobb was so racist that he shocked other racists in a time when racism was chic.

Cobb once stepped on fresh pavement and then slapped a black construction worker who had protested Cobb's damaging his handiwork.

The worst incident came in 1912 at Hilltop Park in New York when a fan heckled Cobb. The two men traded insults, but Cobb went berserk when the man called him a half nigger. Cobb ran 12 rows into the stands and beat the man. Cobb was suspended indefinitely.

No. 3: He is one of the best coaches in the game, but Doug Collins was too high strung to hold a job for long. Once Pistons forward Scot Pollard accidentally stumbled over an electrical cord of a Stairmaster that Collins was using. The coach laced into Pollard until the player threw up his hands as if to say, "What did I do?" His worst transgression was the constant belittling of his players.

Once, mild-mannered Terry Mills squared up on Collins and said, "The only thing that is preventing me from kicking your ass now is a paycheck."

The player tension climaxed midway through the 1997-1998 season when players Grant Hill and Joe Dumars told Collins he needed to lay off the players. Following the next game after that meeting, Collins broke down in tears in the locker room. He had reached his melting point and was fired soon afterward.

DREW | **No. 1:** Terry, how can anybody not have the Georgia Peach as the No. 1 jerk (and that's a word I use charitably in this instance) for his absolute lack of a social conscience? He could be ranked first, second, and third on this list because he was an unapologetic racist. You honor his accomplishments (3,900 hits as a Tiger), but you must also recognize his flaws. There have been numerous idiots, criminals, and ne'er-do-wells within the local sports fraternity, but it's impossible for anyone to measure up to Cobb's social ills.

No. 2: Denny McLain wasn't a racist, merely a crook. This was one cat that used up his nine lives after spending six years in federal prison for stealing from the pension fund of a company that went bankrupt 18 months after he bought it. McLain's prior sins were always forgiven in Detroit, even an earlier two-and-a-half-year prison stay for racketeering. But a working man's town like Detroit couldn't tolerate the idea of somebody bilking the fruits of an hourly worker's long and arduous labors.

No. 3:   Russ Thomas, the Lions general manager (1966–1989), happily wore the villainous dark hat in contract negotiations. He became Public Enemy No. 1 for Lions' fans dismayed over how every good player the Lions had turned spiteful against the organization, because the star players didn't appreciate Thomas's hard-line approach, distributing players' salaries with an eye dropper. What was gained alienating your star players like running back Billy Sims, receiver Ron Jessie, or defensive tackle Doug English? Thomas always justified his actions, saying he was merely articulating his owner's wishes. What a crock! He wasn't a crook so he doesn't deserve higher recognition in this indistinguishable hall of Detroit sports shame.

# What's the tougher job in Detroit sports— Wings' goalie or Lions' quarterback?

DREW Has a Lions quarterback ever assumed verb form in this town when describing one's ineptitude? I don't recall workers in the auto assembly lines telling the guy who screwed up the brakes saying that he really "Mitchelled" that job or that he "Batched" that steering assembly. But Detroiters would often categorize one's clumsiness with the referendum that he really "Chevledaed" that one, in recognition of one of the more maligned athletes in Detroit history—Wings goalie Tim Chevledae.

Detroit is so tough on goalies that, arguably, the best goalie on the planet the last 10 years was roundly booed as he struggled in the first two games of the Wings' 2002 Stanley Cup playoff push.

Dominik Hasek came here in the summer of 2001 in a blockbuster trade with Buffalo. Hasek demanded liberation from the financially strapped Sabres, wanting to play for a serious Stanley Cup contender. The Wings acquired him, paying him $8 million in base pay and an extra $2 million in bonuses. Hasek's job was simple—lead the Wings to the Cup.

But the Wings lost their first two games—at home—against Vancouver in the first round. Hasek surrendered five goals in Game 2, including three goals on the Canucks' first 10 shots on goal, and was booed off the ice following the Wings' 5-2 loss. The man had become the Wings' "bounced Czech" as I wrote in the next day's *Free Press*.

Now that's some nasty stuff, Terry!

Here was the greatest goalie in the game, yet the overriding mood among Wings fans was that Buffalo stuck the city with a lemon.

The Lions have never had anything remotely close to greatness taking snaps during our lifetime. Mediocrity basically gets what it deserves, but the way Hasek was treated after those first two games told you that reputations mean diddly in this city when you're expected to deliver. The quality of the Wings' goalies the last 40 years has been much better than the quality of the Lions quarterbacks over that time span, magnifying the pressure on them to perform to that level.

TERRY Let's go back to 1995 when Scott Mitchell quarterbacked the Lions. He was a big, strong, and handsome guy.

But he heard boos every step he took at the Pontiac Silverdome. Fans threw things at him, called him a wuss, and filled the lines on sports talk radio trying to think of ways to run him out of town.

By the way, that was the year he set Lions' season records for passing yards (4,338) and touchdowns (32) while leading the Lions (10-6) to the playoffs. Two years later he led the Lions to their last playoff appearance. The following season he lost his job to Charlie Batch, who became Lions fans' next whipping boy.

There is no question Lions quarterback is the toughest sports job in Detroit. Here is a guy having a career season, and the lynch mob is formed outside of his workplace. I remember talking to Lions quarterback Gary Danielson, who said the expectations are insane although he claims it never bothered him.

The last Lions quarterback people liked here was Bobby Layne, who helped win the Lions' last championship in 1957. But he was run out of town by the organization a year later.

Since Layne we've run through Eric Hipple, Milt Plum, Karl Sweetan, Chuck Long, Bill Munson, Rodney Peete, Joey Harrington, and countless others. And do you want to know what they all had in common around here?

They were the greatest quarterbacks in the world as backups. But they were all bums in the eyes of fans as starters.

Of course, one playoff victory in five decades does tend to set people off around here.

Do you remember the early 1990s when coach Wayne Fontes struggled to name a quarterback each week, debating over Erik Kramer, Andre Ware, and Peete?

We all wanted whoever was not starting to play. And when he was sent in, we started booing him within minutes.

I remember talking to Harrington's father when the Lions drafted his son. I told him it was a very tough job. He was concerned, but said his son could handle whatever Detroit fans threw at him because he had high expectations also.

I am sure he has rethought that, because this is a job nobody can handle.

 # What was the biggest gamble ever in Detroit sports?

TERRY I could not decide whether to put the hiring of Lions president Matt Millen as the biggest blunder or biggest gamble.

It was both. But let's look at the circumstances of Millen's hiring. The Lions were at least a mediocre team when Chicago Bears kicker Paul Edinger hit the 54-yard field goal that knocked them out of the playoffs.

The Lions fan base was tired of making the playoffs every odd year and getting drummed in the first round. They were tired of missing the playoffs the other seasons. William Clay Ford Sr. finally listened to his son, Bill Ford Jr., and hired Millen to take over the organization.

Junior even said he would stake his reputation on Millen.

But Millen had no front-office experience. He had won four Super Bowl rings on three different teams as a player.

So what? I don't see anyone hiring former Piston John Salley for the front office after he won championships with the Pistons, Chicago Bulls, and Los Angeles Lakers.

Millen understood players because he played in the league. But he came in as a television analyst with Fox. He had relationships in the league, and the Fords gambled those relationships would pay off. However, Millen visited other teams as a friend in television. He was now the enemy, and no one was interested in helping him.

Millen also did not understand that you must carry yourself a certain way to be president. During his tenure Millen used a derogatory terms for gays in a heated exchange with Kansas City Chiefs wide receiver Johnnie Morton, whom Millen had cut. He was fined $200,000 for not interviewing minority candidates and called one of his players a devout coward on a Chicago radio interview.

This was a gamble that did not work. Millen is 21-59 in five seasons and hired former Tampa Bay Bucs defensive line coach Rod Marinelli in January 2006—his third coach in five years. And have you noticed how Millen is infatuated with the letter M?

Millen has hired Marty Mornhinweg, Steve Mariucci, and Marinelli. Who's next? Mickey Mouse?

He is no longer Matt Millen. He is Miller Lite. He has given the Lions the same bad taste, just half the victories.

> **"He is no longer Matt Millen. He is Miller Lite. He has given the Lions the same bad taste, just half the victories."**

DREW | Didn't you read the question, Foster? It says "gamble." Gamble implies the chance, albeit rare, of winning. You think Millen has a chance at winning?

What was Mayo Smith thinking when he flirted with the idea of moving centerfielder Mickey Stanley to shortstop for the 1968 World Series against St. Louis? A manager doesn't mess with anything that's worked flawlessly for the previous six months, but Smith's actions were motivated primarily from loyalty. He knew that Al Kaline had to be in the lineup every day. It just wasn't right that the single most recognizable symbol of the Tigers' franchise for the previous 15 years would sit on the bench for his first World Series.

Kaline had fractured his wrist two months earlier, forcing Smith to shift Jim Northrup from center to right field and place the athletically versatile Stanley in center field.

And there wasn't a drop-off in performance. The Tigers rolled through the American League that season for their first pennant in 23 years. But the Tigers needed Kaline's bat against the Cards, and Smith thought replacing the offensively challenged Ray Oyler at shortstop with Stanley might work—even though Stanley had never before played the position.

Can you imagine, Terry, the heat Smith would have endured if Stanley bobbled a grounder in the late innings that a vacuum cleaner with a glove like Oyler would have swept up and it cost the Tigers a game?

That could have been a fireable offense, and he was the AL Manager of the Year in 1968. That would have made for an interesting parlay, wouldn't it?

I defy anybody to provide evidence of another manager or coach voluntarily making such a radical positional change on the eve of a championship series. But it just shows that fearlessness is an essential component in success. Smith understood that there is no reward without some measure of risk. That's become Mayo's baseball legacy.

 # What was the biggest blunder in Detroit sports?

DREW You know something is so obviously and ridiculously wrong when someone who doesn't even have the slightest grasp of football strategy recognizes the mistake.

My wife, Karen, called me on my cell phone just minutes after I left the press box at Illinois's Memorial Stadium in 2002 with just one simple question.

"What the hell was he thinking not taking the ball?" she wondered.

She wasn't alone.

The legacy of Marty Mornhinweg's brief two-year hiccup as Lions head coach was determined that cold, blustery November afternoon in Champaign, Illinois, when he took the wind after winning the overtime coin flip against the Chicago Bears. The decision didn't make sense under normal circumstances, but magnifying its stupidity was taking the wind and going on defense immediately after your defense had been on the field for the last seven minutes of the fourth quarter and had surrendered the game-tying touchdown.

You never voluntarily give away the ball when it's sudden death and the first team that scores wins. Even the Bears at the 50-yard line for the coin flip couldn't contain their glee, giddily bouncing off the field like a kid that just snatched the last cupcake unbeknownst to his big brother.

And, of course, you know how this story ended. The Bears took the ball, and even with a pretty strong breeze blowing in their faces, they nonetheless moved down the field against an exhausted Lions defense. Kicker Paul Edinger booted a 32-yard field goal for a 20-17 Chicago victory, extending the Lions' road losing streak to 14 games.

Mornhinweg's rationale for his choice made even less sense. His justification was that Tom Landry, Bill Parcells, and Dan Reeves had done similar things in similar circumstances. But there's just one flaw with that theory—*those guys won or at least coached in Super Bowls, which meant they had reputable teams, thus minimizing the risks!*

TERRY | The Pistons were five seconds from beating the Boston Celtics when Larry Bird missed a shot and all the Pistons had to do to win was inbound the ball. They led 107-106 after an exhausting Game 5 of the 1987 Eastern Conference Finals at Boston Gardens.

The Pistons ran down the court in celebration, and Isiah Thomas did not see coach Chuck Daly's frantic demand for a timeout.

Thomas grabbed the ball and threw the worst pass in Detroit sports.

Blunder one was throwing the ball to teammate Bill Laimbeer toward his own basket. And blunder two was not seeing Larry Bird lurking in the weeds. Bird intercepted it and just before stepping out of bounds tossed a pass to a streaking Dennis Johnson. Johnson's twisting layup sank the Pistons 108-107 and turned a sure 3-2 Pistons lead in the best-of-seven series into Boston's advantage at 3-2.

Boston won the series in seven games. The home team won each game, and I am convinced the Celtics could not have won in the Silverdome. The lapse in judgment cost the Pistons the series and a chance to be mentioned along with the Los Angeles Lakers and Celtics as one of the elite teams of the 1980s.

It is a pass that haunts Thomas today even though the Pistons rebounded the following season to advance to three straight NBA Finals and win two titles.

The pass led to the Pistons' defeat. And it led to Vinnie Johnson and Adrian Dantley bumping heads in Game 7, and Dennis Rodman saying, "Bird would just be another player if he were black," which got pinned on Thomas when Thomas agreed with Rodman.

It caused Thomas great embarrassment, and he had to defend himself as pundits called him a racist. It was a domino effect of anguish that all started with the worst pass in Detroit history.

What movie title
would you give each of the
four Detroit professional
sports franchises and why?

DREW | *The Good, the Bad, the Ugly, and the Underachieving*—rated PG-55 for those 55 and over who were old enough to witness the last Lions' championship. Clint Eastwood stars as the renegade mute hired to become the Lions' next coach. His silence blows team president Matt Millen away at the job interview. Millen insists that the Eastwood character possesses the right touch for coaching this team, especially during the postgame press conferences following another embarrassing loss. Because nobody has any answers for the franchise's continued ineptitude, there's no need for any verbalization.

Field of Dreams—rated PG-13 for those 13 consecutive years that the Tigers have gone without a winning season. Kevin Costner stars as an Iowa farmer who grew up a Detroit Tigers fan and who now suddenly hears voices in his cornfield. "If you build it, Pudge will come." Costner constructs a baseball diamond on his farm with the belief that it will attract quality free agents to the Tigers, but actually it was a reminder of the arrival of his 200-pound mother-in-law. His family and friends brand him insane. He's immediately committed to a mental hospital with the assurances that he'll be released once the Tigers finally play a meaningful game in late September. He's still hospitalized as of 2010.

Rain Man, Odd Man Rush—rated PG-10 for the 10 years from 1995 to 2004 in which the Red Wings were the NHL gold standard.

Dustin Hoffman won an Academy Award as the idiot savant who couldn't perform the simplest tasks, but could master the intricacies involved in becoming the greatest hockey coach of all time. Hoffman's antics didn't make sense and often frustrated the bejabbers out of his players, but he somehow knew the right computations at the right time to get the right results for the Red Wings—three Stanley Cup championships in a six-year span. And all the man ever said on the bench was, "Wapner on at seven."

L.B.: The Extra Terrestrial—rated R for ridiculous. Larry Brown stars as the curious alien who mystically comes to Earth to fulfill his destiny as a vagabond NBA head coach. Everywhere he goes, he brings instant magic only to just as quickly move on elsewhere. He has a knack for leaving just when his team is ready to slide downward. He comes to coach the Detroit Pistons and in his first year gets his first NBA coaching championship. But in the middle of his second season with the Pistons, the alien receives a message from his homeland, "L.B. Come home. Call your agent." He leaves the Pistons after two seasons in another melodramatic parting, but the Pistons perform even better in his absence.

TERRY | *Hey! Hey! Hockeytown*—by Disney Films. Gene Hackman plays Scotty Bowman, the strange coach who talked a lot, but said nothing. He's the hero Detroit craved. "Rain Man" meets Steve Yzerman and turns a franchise that used to drink too much and lose too much into a winner. Keanu Reeves co-stars as Steve Yzerman, a small-town boy who learns about leadership in the big jungle of professional sports.

It looks like our hero is about to fail when Bowman decides he's seen enough and wants to trade Yzerman. But fans cheer for Yzerman's return during a tearful scene at Joe Louis Arena, and he rallies to save the day.

Of course, this film might seem a little unrealistic. There is actually a happy ending here, which Detroit fans are not used to. Watch as players from other teams want to make Detroit a destination and watch as Bowman and Yzerman, who often had a troubled relationship, hug and become buddies at the end.

Bad Boys—by HBO and starring the entire cast of *Oz*. We watch as the Pistons win titles and leave bodies in their wake. You never know what member of the Chicago Bulls or Milwaukee Bucks will end up lame and bloodied.

Then comes the major clashes with Michael Jordan, the greatest player of them all. Joe Dumars, played by former NFL star Ronnie Lott, plays the best defense in the land against M.J. But finally M.J. wins and destroys the Pistons, who go through lean times.

It is so bad you can hear crickets buzzing at The Palace.

But then a new group of Pistons comes on the scene. They are younger, faster, and friendlier, and they make basketball important in Detroit again. Watch as Chauncey Billups, Rasheed Wallace, and Ben Wallace bring pride to the red, white, and blue again. And the former Bad Boys applaud from the sidelines in wheelchairs and walkers.

And Dumars gets the final laugh over Jordan when he swindles Rip Hamilton from him in a trade that sends Jerry Stackhouse to the Washington Wizards. Dumars ends up as Executive of the Year while Jordan is thrown into the streets and begs for pennies from Pistons fans.

Loveable Losers by Hard Luck Pictures. People in Detroit scream at, stomp on, and ridicule the Lions. They throw eggs at them and march in protest about the awful product on the field. But fans still love them.

John Candy and Ruben Studdard, the fat *American Idol* singer, play two overweight players who become frustrated by the front-office mistakes that make the team around them pathetic. They try to send the message to team president Matt Millen (Burt Reynolds) that he is incompetent and should be removed. But they can't get the message through to Millen in this comedy. This one features nonstop laughter as Millen and the players play the dozens on each other in the dressing room and in the media.

And their coach, played by Barney Fife, sits and watches helplessly as his dressing room turns into an inferno.

And, of course, those wacky Lions fans come all dressed in blue and white face paint thinking their team will turn the corner after every game. But they leave Ford Field cursing.

Lost—from the producers of Ship Wrecked Films, the entire grown-up cast of *The Bad News Bears* reunites to play the roles of our bumbling and stumbling Tigers. Watch balls roll between their legs and bounce off their heads for home runs. Watch thinning crowds grab their heads and moan in anger as the Tigers lose game after game after game.

Who comes in and saves the day?

Unfortunately nobody. This team is truly lost.

Where are you, Tigers? Didn't you use to play at Tiger Stadium and Comerica Park? Didn't you use to contend for division titles and win World Series titles? Didn't you use to be an elite franchise?

You sure did. The problem is an entire generation of baseball fans only know you as losers. They barely pay attention to you.

They consider you lost.

GRID-IRON
GRIDLOCK

# Who had the biggest impact on football in the state of Michigan?

DREW | Michigan State president John Hannah thought he could raise his land grant college's profile through football when he hired Clarence "Biggie" Munn as the Spartans' head football coach in 1948.

And Munn became the greatest single force in college football in the state of Michigan because he pushed the integration of football among northern schools even further. Michigan State became the first northern college football program to aggressively recruit Southern black football stars who, at the time, could only attend black colleges such as Grambling if they wished to remain close to home.

The Spartans opened a door, creating opportunities and selling the university.

Former Michigan State athletic director Clarence Underwood once told me the story of how he found out about MSU. It was January 1, 1954, and Underwood, a Georgia native, was returning home from an Army tour of duty when he noticed something on television. He saw all of these black guys playing for this school he had never heard of in the Rose Bowl. Underwood was impressed. He told me that at that very moment, he decided he would attend Michigan State. He graduated from MSU in 1961.

Munn's Spartans won the national championship in 1952, the year before they officially joined the Big Ten. His seven-year coaching record at MSU was 54-9-2, including a 28-game winning streak from 1950 to 1953.

Munn's presence was felt long after he left the sidelines in 1954, becoming the Spartans' athletic director. Around 20 percent of the Spartans team was black in the late 1950s, but the Southern talent floodgates busted open in the 1960s, and Michigan State developed a cooperative with Southern coaches like Alabama's Bear Bryant and Clemson's Frank Howard, who weren't able to recruit black players.

They would steer a black player to Michigan State, and if there was a white player that the Spartans couldn't enroll because of academic questions, they would steer him southward.

That was the deal with Joe Namath. The Pennsylvania native wanted to play for the Spartans in 1963 but didn't have the grades for admission. Michigan State coach Duffy Daugherty contacted Bryant, and Namath became a star for the Crimson Tide. Bryant returned the favor. Linebacker Charlie Thornhill hailed from Roanoke, Virginia, and wanted to play for Alabama, but blacks couldn't go there, so he wound up in East Lansing.

Michigan State remained a national football power until the late 1960s when Southern schools finally integrated.

But it was Munn's vision nearly 20 years earlier that started the movement.

TERRY Some of you are old enough to remember when Michigan State reigned as king of football in our state. Then Bo Schembechler took over at the University of Michigan, and we haven't heard much from the Spartans since.

In 21 seasons, Schembechler was 17-4 against the Spartans and put the Wolverines on the map with historic games against his mentor Woody Hayes and Ohio State. This isn't to say Michigan's program was in shambles when Schembechler took over in 1969. But they'd won only one Big Ten title the last 18 years.

Schembechler came in like a lion. He upset Ohio State 24-12 in his first season and won or shared five of the next six Big Ten titles on his way to a total of 13. That game in 1969 sparked the 10-year war

Yes, everyone knows Bo, but did he do the most for football in Michigan?

and turned the Michigan–Ohio State rivalry into one of the most intense in the country. The exposure from that game made this a national event, and recruits from across the country got to see the Scarlet and Grey battle the Maize and Blue.

Schembechler put Michigan on the map when television was growing into one of the country's favorite pastimes. Future players such as Jamie Morris fell in love with the program just by seeing the famous winged helmets on television.

Chances are if you are strolling around, you will see someone wearing a Michigan T-shirt or hat. It does not matter if you are in Detroit or Denver, Ann Arbor or Alabama. Michigan is one of the most exposed programs in the nation, and the spark came from Schembechler.

During my junior year at Cass Tech High School in 1976, Schembechler came by to recruit running back Harlan Huckleby. It created a buzz around the school, because Schembechler was the biggest sports icon in the state. We spent the entire day trying to get a glimpse of him, and his visit was even bigger than a walk-through by the President of the United States.

Schembechler won 234 games in his career. Only a handful of men have been able to do that. He was terrible in bowl games (5-12), never won a national title, and was one of the most stubborn men in modern sports history. But he turned Michigan into one of the top five watched programs in the nation.

Michigan fans own this state because they root for the best program. Yeah, they are arrogant, and their "Go Blue!" chants are annoying. But they can walk big and talk big because of Bo Schembechler—the godfather of Michigan football.

 **Who was the best player in college football in the state of Michigan who should have won the Heisman?**

DREW Lorenzo White's name still ranks among the top all-time rushers in college football, but what makes the former Michigan State star stand out is that he's one of only two top 10 career rushers who doesn't have a Heisman Trophy on his college resumé. (Texas's Cedric Benson is the other.)

There wasn't a better college player in 1987, and there certainly wasn't anybody more important to his team's success that season than White.

He finished fourth in Heisman voting that year.

Notre Dame receiver and kick returner Tim Brown won the award based on two early-season punt returns for touchdowns in primetime nationally televised games against Michigan and Michigan State. That was ridiculous enough, but Syracuse quarterback Don McPherson and Holy Cross two-way player Gordie Lockbaum finished second and third, respectively.

White was cheated. He led the nation in rushing two years earlier when he became the first Big Ten rusher in history to gain more than 2,000 yards in a season. So it's not like he was an unknown commodity coming into his senior season in 1987.

The nation supposedly loves the team that comes out of virtually nowhere for a special season, and that was the Spartans in 1987. They won the Big Ten championship, going to the Rose Bowl for the first time in more than 20 years. And White was the difference-maker in coach George Perles's ball-control, field-position philosophy. Perles loved running backs who could carry the workload, and he ran White like a pack mule. In the Big Ten championship-clinching game against Indiana, White ran the ball a school-record 56 times.

White rushed for 1,572 yards that season and was a first-team All-American.

He finished his career with 4,887 yards, a mark that at the time was the second highest in Big Ten history behind Ohio State's great Archie Griffin, who became the only player to win back-to-back Heisman Trophies.

That slight forever convinced me that the Heisman was more about hype than history.

TERRY | Imagine Ron Kramer doing the same things today that he did in the middle 1950s? He not only would have won a Heisman Trophy, but he would be an ESPN poster boy.

Kramer is Michigan's greatest athlete on and off the football field. One reason he did not win the Heisman in 1956 was because he lacked the star power of Notre Dame's Paul Horning. We all know the Heisman is about hype and is a bigger popularity contest than the Miss America Pageant.

Michigan was never big into hyping its players. But there was plenty to crow about Kramer. Kramer was a consensus All-American in 1955 and 1956 as a receiver. But he also played defensive end, quarterback, running back, and kicker—often in the same game. And we thought Charles Woodson was special.

Kramer was praised for catching and running the football, but Michigan coach Bennie Oosterbaan said Kramer's blocking and tackling were his most important assets. And we know winning football games back in that day was all about fundamentals and grit.

Kramer had all of that, and he could outrun anyone in the country.

But that's not all. He captained the basketball team his senior season and set the school record for career points scored (1,124), a mark that has since been broken. He often walked over to the track after spring football practice and competed in the high jump. Despite weighing 230 pounds, he was able to hurl his six-foot-four frame into the air and over the bar.

So what does this have to do with football? Nothing. But it shows what type of athlete Kramer was. He won nine letters in three years, and if Michigan had known how to market players better, Kramer would have won the Heisman with ease.

In 1955 he finished eighth in the Heisman balloting and lacked the catchy name of Ohio State running back Hopalong Cassidy, and the following season he finished sixth.

Today, Michigan players know Kramer as "The Apple Man." Players used to get an apple a day from former players when Kramer played. He continues the tradition and provides apples for players, coaches, and support staff.

"Who is that old man?" players often asked.

He simply is one of Michigan's greatest athletes and a man who should own a Heisman Trophy.

# Who's been better for Michigan football— Bo Schembechler or Lloyd Carr?

TERRY I am not going to bore you with statistics. We all know what Bo Schembechler meant to the game of football. He was one of the most influential men in college football history. You cannot say the same about Lloyd Carr.

This debate isn't even close, and I know you, Drew, are going to talk about Carr and the 1997 national championship. And I want to remind you that it was a *shared* championship. There is no guarantee Michigan was better than Nebraska, although that is a nice feather in Carr's cap.

But what have you stuck-up Michigan alumni been talking about ever since?

Fire Lloyd Carr!

Boodini, I find it hard to believe you are going to support Lloyd Carr, a guy you attack during every waking breath. The guy only tolerates you, because there would be too many witnesses for him to do what he really wants to do to you during press conferences.

The reason Carr can win his eight to 10 games per season is because of the foundation laid down by Schembechler. And you are right. Schembechler never won a national title, and his bowl record was terrible. But he was a couple points from winning titles in 1973 and 1974. A 10-10 tie against Ohio State ruined it in 1973. Michigan was clearly the better team and would have won if you had overtime like you do today. And the Wolverines lost the national title the following season by losing 12-10 to OSU.

Yes, he did not win it. But Schembechler was in the hunt for it more than Carr is.

Here is how much respect you give Carr. You blue bloods have been trying to talk him into quitting as head coach and becoming the athletic director for the past three years.

You believe he is past his time and could help the program better through fund-raising. You are one of those guys who believes the only reason Carr has his job is because of 1997. He is 73-26 since the national title, which is great. But that is not good enough for you Blue fans.

You secretly long for the Bo Schembechler days. He was the guy who made you important and he made Carr's job much easier.

D R E W | When Lloyd Carr sees this, he'll probably lapse into apoplectic shock.

Yes, I'm giving him credit for something, Terry, simply because if you're not moving forward, you're sliding backward.

As important as Bo Schembechler was in raising the Michigan football program from the ashes of the 1960s, Carr's contributions were greater because the program's objectives had to change along with the college football landscape. It's about recruiting now. It's about television exposure. And, yes, it's about contending for national championships.

College football was more insular during Schembechler's time. Winning the Big Ten championship and getting to the Rose Bowl was all that mattered around here then. The mythical national championship was frowned upon. It was beneath Michigan's reputation to desire something that, in its mind, was inferior to striving for the Rose Bowl.

But 1997 changed all of that.

Can Lloyd Carr compete with Bo Schembechler's success at Michigan?

Carr's job security was tenuous at best. He was entering his third year as the Wolverines' head coach, ascending to the job in the aftermath of Gary Moeller's unceremonious ouster in April 1995 following an embarrassing night of inebriation at a suburban Detroit restaurant.

The university athletic department power brokers believed Carr, Moeller's defensive coordinator, was overmatched, and they brought in new athletic director Tom Goss in 1997 with one primary directive—fire basketball coach Steve Fisher and Carr.

Fisher was ousted in October 1997 when the NCAA investigated alleged improprieties.

But Carr used his critics' skepticism as motivation that season, challenging his players to imagine the unthinkable—going unbeaten and winning the national championship, not just the Big Ten crown. It opened a new door for Michigan football fans.

The Wolverines went 12-0 and shared the national championship with Nebraska, its first national title since 1948.

Michigan realized that there was nothing wrong with aiming high. Carr stopped the regional thinking that was Schembechler's strength.

 # Who was Michigan's best No. 1 in football?

DREW | The No. 1 jersey symbolizes style as much as substance, but it also is a testament to a player's growth over the length of his time at Michigan. Braylon Edwards satisfied all three criteria better than anybody else who wore that special number. "The Big Easy" was the best combination of size, strength, and speed ever in a Michigan receiver.

Edwards has seven season and career Michigan receiving records—among them, career receptions (252), season receptions (97), most yardage in a career (3,541), most yardage in a season (1,330), and career touchdowns (39).

Edwards didn't initially understand the importance of having the number. He thought it was all show when he asked to switch from No. 80 to No. 1 before his junior season. He didn't appreciate the responsibility that came with the number. Edwards thought getting the number marked the destination, but it was really only the start of the process. There were stretches when he didn't practice hard that junior season. He sulked when Lloyd Carr not only benched him, but publicly challenged his commitment in the media—something that Carr had never done before with one of his players.

The message finally sunk in as Edwards prepared for his senior season. He cropped the Afro hairstyle down to a more conservative, shorter look. Gone were the baggy jeans on game day and in their place were nice suits that conveyed a businesslike attitude. Edwards evolved into one of Michigan football's best leaders, and sometimes that deserves as much if not more recognition than what's done on the field.

And let's not forget that he was the highest drafted receiver in Michigan history, going third overall in the 2005 NFL draft to the Cleveland Browns.

TERRY Anthony Carter came to Michigan at the wrong time. He came in at the height of the Michigan "three yards and a cloud of dust" offense. And he came in at a time when Michigan coach Bo Schembechler did not believe in hyping people for the Heisman Trophy.

In 1982 Carter was the most dominant wide receiver in college football, but he did not come close to winning a Heisman Trophy. He should have. He finished fourth in the voting, finishing only behind quarterbacks and wide receivers.

Ask Michigan fans who the Wolverines' best player was regardless of number. And nearly half of them will tell you it was A.C.

This is how great Carter is. All you need are his initials to know who he is.

If you say B.E. is returning to Michigan, most fans would fear they are rehiring former basketball coach Brian Ellerbe. They would not even think of Braylon Edwards.

In four seasons Carter caught 161 passes for 3,076 yards and 37 touchdowns. Of course Edwards came through and broke many of A.C.'s records. But Carter had Steve Smith and Rick Leach throwing to him. Edwards had John Navarre and Chad Henne, both better passers.

Edwards ran in a pro-style offense. Carter spent most of his time blocking because Schembechler believed only three things could happen when teams passed. And two of them were bad.

But Carter still enjoyed 14 100-yard games receiving and was the Big Ten's Most Valuable Player in 1982. That same season he became just the Big Ten's eighth three-time All-American.

One of the most famous touchdowns in Michigan history was the buzzer-beater 55-yard touchdown pass from John Wrangler to Carter that beat Indiana 27-21 in 1979 that sent a homecoming crowd into a frenzy.

Carter was a threat every time he took the field. And that No. 1 and those high socks made him look faster and more elusive.

Carter endeared himself even more to Detroit fans when he helped the Michigan Panthers win a USFL title with brilliant kick and punt returns.

Did "Spartan Bob," the timekeeper, hose Michigan in its 2001 loss to Michigan State?

TERRY | I suppose you didn't notice when time stood still. You didn't notice that Michigan State quarterback Jeff Smoker still had the ball in his hand with one second left on the clock.

You didn't notice how every tick of the clock in that game marched off like a military unit until the final one?

Sparty Bob did something current Michigan State coach John L. Smith was unable to do. He beat Michigan with a slow hand.

It was the first 60-minute, one-second game of this storied rivalry. The extra tick of the clock cost Michigan a shot at a national championship game, and it caused bedlam in East Lansing among Spartans fans.

We debated this game for weeks on talk radio, and it made people forget the tragic events of 9/11. That is how fierce the arguments were.

Yes, Michigan made mistakes. Cornerback Jeremy LeSueur made a mistake when he put his hands in the facemask of MSU receiver Charles Rogers and was called for personal foul penalty on fourth and 16 on the Spartans' last drive.

But football is filled with mistakes. That is what happens during the ebb and flow of a college football game. The bottom line is players should rely on grown-ups to do their jobs. This was not the case when an obviously pro-MSU fan/clock operator gave his school the hookup.

This is a debate that will rage forever. I've received several emails from Spartans fans who ran their VCRs frame by frame and said Smoker got the spike down in time. And I've heard from the same number of Michigan fans who slowed the final play down frame by frame and swear he did not.

Obviously, Michigan and Michigan State fans do not shop at the same Best Buy.

Michigan coach Lloyd Carr was criticized for saying his players deserved better. I agree. The Wolverines did deserve better. The problem is Michigan complains so much you tend to ignore it even when the school really gets shafted.

DREW Grab your Maize and Blue Kleenex, Terry, and wipe your nose from the crocodile tears you're shedding. I say this as a Michigan alum and someone who grew up as a diehard Wolverines fan, but Michigan fans are the biggest whiners in sports. Michigan has never lost a football game. It's never happened. Defeat was always the fault of the refs or, in this case, the timekeeper. Every loss was part of this grand conspiracy that within the rationally challenged thought process of the maniacal Michigan fan was surpassed only by the Kennedy assassination.

There's a rule of thumb in clock-managed competitions. Never put yourself in a position where you're potentially at the mercy of outside factors. Terry, it doesn't matter if a super slow-motion review reveals that the stadium clock stayed at 00:01 a millisecond longer than it should have, the Wolverines lost that game earlier on that drive when a stupid penalty by

> "Never put yourself in a position where you're potentially at the mercy of outside factors."

Michigan cornerback Jeremy LeSueur gave the Spartans life when they were toast.

On fourth down and 16 at midfield with 1:18 remaining in the game, the Wolverines broke up a desperate pass from quarterback Jeff Smoker and thought they won the game. But the officials flagged LeSueur for a personal foul, the grabbing of Charles Rogers's facemask—a 15-yard penalty that gave Michigan State the ball at the Michigan 35.

The game should have been over, but Michigan has nobody to blame but itself. But instead of taking accountability for their own fate, the Wolverines cried robbery.

Get a life. Get a clue. It all balances out. Sometimes, the breaks roll your way, and other times, they slide through your grasp like running water. That's why teams can only worry about matters that they can control—like not having a brain freeze at a critical juncture and committing a boneheaded penalty. So grab a Kleenex, Michigan fan, wipe your runny nose, and shut your running mouth.

 **You are starting a new Division I-A college football program in the state of Michigan. Do you want Lloyd Carr or John L. Smith taking the reins?**

TERRY We are starting from scratch. We don't have to worry about the Michigan State demons, and we are not building off the Michigan tradition.

MSU coach John L. Smith is the obvious choice.

He is flawed as a coach. He needs to learn clock management and must be surrounded by a great staff.

But here is what Smith has that Carr does not. He has innovation and works the spread offense better than most. That is the way to go in modern football.

The athletes in college football get better every year. It makes no sense putting them in stagnant systems where they pound the opponent for 60 minutes.

Smith believes in doing it the easy way by spreading the talent all over the field and letting them pitch and catch. He has running backs going against defenses with six and seven men in the box. For all of his flaws elsewhere, he is an offensive genius.

Besides, Smith has already built programs. He has won six conference championships in Conference USA, the Big Sky, and the Big West.

He is the winningest coach in school history at Idaho State.

In 1993 his team led the nation in Division I-AA in scoring (47.5 points a game) and total offense (532.0 yards).

Utah State enjoyed two winning seasons in the 15 years before Smith's arrival. Smith had winning seasons in two of three years and guided the Aggies to the Humanitarian Bowl in 1997.

And finally he built Louisville into a power—and that is a basketball school. You know how difficult it is to win in football at a basketball school. But Smith put the Cardinals on the map in football. He helped plant the seeds for the school to move from Conference USA to the Big East. The team finished 1-10 the year before Smith arrived. They were 7-5 in Smith's first season.

What has Carr built?

He continued the fine tradition at Michigan. But let's be honest. We don't know if the man is a great coach or if he is in a great system. Michigan will win no matter who coaches there. You can run a spread, Wishbone, or T-bone, and it does not matter.

If you are building a program from scratch, why not hire a guy who has already built a program from scratch?

DREW | What do you think the "L" stands for, Terry? Longshot! I must concede that all of this Carr gushing is turning my stomach, but given the choices available, how can you not want Carr taking over a new program with his background?

Don't bore me with gimmicks. John L. Smith has his funky little offense, flooding the scoreboard with points—except, of course, in the fourth quarter, if the second half of the 2005 season was any indication. But if I'm starting a program, I want a concentration on the basics. The most important factor in Michigan's consistency over the last 35 years was continuity with the offensive line. All of its coaches understood that keeping the offensive line strong makes it easier to cope with the inevitable turnover at quarterback.

Carr would best understand that his most important hire would be his first offensive line coach.

Can John L. Smith build a football program from scratch or is he just a gimmick man?

Building a successful program from scratch takes time, but more importantly, it requires a firm commitment in your strategy. I've always believed that Smith's spread offense philosophy was based more out of reflex than resolve. It creates attention, builds buzz, and hopefully sells tickets in a hurry. But winning programs aren't constructed with ease, and they're built upward from the trenches—and in football that's the offensive line.

I'm taking Carr, and I'm also ending this debate quickly before I get sick.

# Will Wayne State ever become a Division II college football power?

DREW It won't happen because neither the local nor university support is there. It's tough enough for a Division II program to succeed in a major metropolitan area because you can only stretch the sports dollar so far, but it's especially challenging in Detroit, which is the home of four professional sports teams and three Division I-A football programs within a 90-mile radius—Michigan, Michigan State, and Eastern Michigan. There's little breathing room for another program to grow and prosper.

It's not a coincidence that the state's top two Division II football programs hail from the Grand Rapids (Grand Valley State) and Flint–Saginaw area (Saginaw Valley State). The areas are big enough to provide the necessary fan support, and those schools are pretty much the only game in town, so sharing the spotlight isn't mandatory.

Also, the infrastructure isn't there. It doesn't help that Wayne State is strictly a commuter school. The student body doesn't hang around campus once the school day is done, and you have to wonder how much the students really care about having a dominating football program. They're probably more inclined to spend a fall Saturday afternoon watching the Wolverines or the Spartans on television than watching their own school play in person.

The university knows that there are far better uses for the school's financial resources than attempting an upgrade of the football program. What does Wayne State gain with such an attempt? Nothing.

TERRY | I was fortunate enough to travel around the GLIAC and talk to people about Wayne State's program. The people who know the league say Wayne State is already on its way to becoming a football power.

And do you know where most of the noise is coming from? It is coming from Grand Valley, Saginaw Valley, and Northwood—the three powers in the conference. They respect Paul Winters, a compassionate coach who is determined to build a winner downtown.

Wayne State has not enjoyed a winning season since 1993, but a lot of the obstacles that prevented it from winning are being erased. The man in charge of changing things is innovative athletic director Rob Fournier. He is putting in the sizzle and removing the fizzle from Wayne State athletics.

He helped raise most of the $1.2 million that the school used to build a new football office and dressing room area underneath Adams Field. Coaches used to keep recruits away from the facilities. That was how bad they were. Now the football offices are a source of pride, and it has led to two of the best recruiting classes in school history. Opponents already say Wayne State has the best athletes in the conference along with Grand Valley and Saginaw Valley. They simply need to learn to play together.

> "[Rob Fournier] is putting in the sizzle and removing the fizzle from Wayne State athletics."

A number of freshmen would have started the 2005 season, but Winters wanted to do it the right way, so he redshirted them and plans to compete for the conference title in 2006.

"We are going to win here," he told me after they lost their final game 28-14 at Hillsdale.

You need to sit down with Winters and talk about what he wants to do. He is convincing. He knows what it takes to win and he is pretty determined.

And he is getting plenty of help from the school. WSU built new dormitories, and the commuter school is getting more of a campus feel. Fournier is building a new basketball and ice hockey arena, and that is going to add excitement to the entire athletic program.

But football is king. Members of the GLIAC want Wayne State to succeed. Officials believe if the Detroit media supports Wayne State, then it will generate more exposure for the entire league. Wayne State is sort of the New York of the GLIAC. Yes, Grand Valley is king, but Detroit's media is much more powerful than that in Grand Rapids.

So, Boodini, when Wayne State becomes a football power, let's do lunch on campus and purchase Wayne State sweatshirts to celebrate a real football power in the city of Detroit.

And, of course, you know I am not talking about the Lions.

# Would Detroit gladly trade its recent professional and collegiate championships for one Lions' Super Bowl win?

TERRY | I've spoken to Detroit fans who said they can die if they get a chance to see the Lions win a Super Bowl. So if people are willing to give their lives to the cause, they'd be willing to trade in championship banners from the Pistons, Red Wings, and Tigers.

The Lions have never been to a Super Bowl. They've won just one playoff game since winning the 1957 NFL championship. There is enough pent-up aggression in this town to power New York City for a decade. Lions fans walk around like a pack of rabid dogs, looking for that elusive title.

When the Lions won their first four games in 1980, radio stations played Queen's "Another One Bites the Dust." There was such a demand that Lions players did a music video.

"Spider Man" Jimmy Allen, Al "Bubba" Baker, and Gary Danielson became cult heroes.

In 1991 this town went into a frenzy when the Lions advanced to the NFC championship game before being throttled by Washington. The days leading up to that game were as magical as the Pistons runs in 1989, 1990, and 2004, and the Red Wings runs in 1997, 1998, and 2002.

The other sports are big, but they are so miniscule in comparison to the Lions. The biggest time of the year in this town is the Lions' season. The second biggest time is the Lions' offseason.

Lion fans are sick. They want this so badly that rooting for this team makes them ill and mentally unstable. They scream and complain about this team in almost the same breath as they embrace and sing its praises.

They want a title just as badly as Cubs fans in Chicago or Browns fans in Cleveland.

But if the Lions ever do succeed in making it to the big game, you will see a bunch of people lying in coffins with smiles on their faces.

DREW | No, no, no—no!!!
I understand how badly Detroit wants a Super Bowl championship. The NFL lords over the other sports, and its championship stage remains the biggest and boldest, but Detroit needs to understand how lucky it is with its far-reaching impact in college and professional sports.

Since 1984, Detroit has had 10 world or national championships in the top six sports—Major League Baseball, the NFL, the NBA, the NHL, and NCAA football and men's basketball. No other city can boast that many titles during one period in so many different sports. Detroit's bragging rights exist in how those 10 championships were spread out over five of the six sports.

Los Angeles has had 12 championships during that same period, divided among four sports,

"No other city can boast that many titles during one period in so many different sports."

but the Lakers are responsible for more than half of those titles with seven NBA championships. Chicago has had eight championships since 1984, but six of those came from the NBA's Bulls during Michael Jordan's reign.

There's a championship balance in Detroit sports (the Red Wings and Pistons are tied for the lead with three championships apiece since 1984) that more than compensates for the Lions winning only one playoff game since their last NFL championship in 1957.

A Lions' berth in the Super Bowl gives Detroit two weeks of exhilaration, considering the pregame buildup and the game itself. But knowing that the Wings and Pistons are likely championship contenders, that Michigan annually goes into every college football season as one of a handful of teams blessed with the opportunity of playing for the national title, and that Tom Izzo has built Michigan State basketball to a level that it's perennially recognized as a serious Final Four contender provides Detroit sports with months of excitement that are priceless.

Instead of trading other teams' successes for one moment of Lions bliss, let's place pressure on the Lions to wake up, wise up, and catch up to everybody else.

Who would you take—
Barry Sanders
or Billy Sims?

DREW | Sims was the Lions' back who best epitomized the Detroit take-no-crap-kick-you-in-the-teeth-while-you're-looking attitude. Sanders made tacklers miss. Sims took them on and then took them out. And that's the guy I want in the backfield in a crucial moment, because I'm more inclined to need three yards to win a game than 30.

To get me those three yards I could trust Billy Sims more than Barry Sanders.

There's the enduring image of Sanders spinning a New England Patriots defender in a full 360-degree circle with an array of jukes and jives. But people too easily forget the play against Houston on November 13, 1983, when Sims encountered an approaching Houston Oilers defensive back. Sims couldn't get past him, so Sims tried drop-kicking the guy. This was football, but this guy thought he was Bruce Lee in a kung-fu movie. Sims gave the tackler a cleat to the face, much to the shock of everyone in the Astrodome that day. Sims was flagged for a personal foul. But those actions sent a strong message to a team that was languishing at 5-5 entering that Houston game. Sims wanted to prove something, and he wouldn't let anything stand in his way.

The Lions lost that day in Houston, but they came together immediately afterward, winning four of the next five games to claim the NFC Central Division championship—the Lions' first title of any kind since their 1957 NFL championship. And it was largely because of Sims's emotional pull within that locker room.

That was always the most frustrating aspect of Sanders's career. His silence often came across as indifference. But you couldn't keep Sims quiet. He openly battled with Lions general manager Russ Thomas regarding his contract. He went as far as signing a contract with the rival United States Football League prior to the 1983 NFL season. That contract was later voided, and Sims returned to the Lions, but the ensuing controversy of his potential departure during the course of the Lions' season didn't dilute his determination—as evidenced by that drop-kick in Houston.

During halftime of the Lions' regular-season finale against Tampa Bay, the Lions announced that Sims had signed a contract extension with the Lions. An arbitrator later ruled the USFL agreement as invalid.

But Sims was only a Lion for eight more games, blowing out a knee at Minnesota on October 21, 1984.

TERRY | What's wrong with making guys miss? That was the strength of Barry Sanders. That is why he lasted 10 seasons and Sims lasted four. It is why Sanders could be the NFL's all-time leading rusher if he so chose.

He averaged 1,573 yards rushing per season, which is the best in NFL history. Sims never rushed for 1,500 yards in his career.

Sanders ran around guys. He dipped and ducked his way to 15,269 yards rushing and 99 touchdowns. He walked away too soon, which angered a number of Lions fans. Many have forgiven him, and they now embrace the Hall of Fame runner.

What's not to like about Sanders? He was only the most exciting runner in NFL history, and he did it behind an average offensive line. Sanders made going to Lions games worthwhile for frustrated Lions fans. Even if the team did not win, fans got to see Sanders take their breath away. They felt as if they were running alongside Sanders in 1997 when he rushed for 2,053 yards.

Which No. 20 makes a run as the top Lion? Billy Sims (left) or Barry Sanders (right)?

Sanders won Rookie of the Year honors in 1988 and was NFL Player of the Year in 1991 and 1997. Sims was a wonderful runner and carried many of Sanders's traits.

But Sanders is a once-in-a-generation runner.

Former Oklahoma State teammate Thurman Thomas once said about Sanders, "He didn't take a big hit. Guys were off balance playing against him. Barry was in a Michael Jordan-like zone."

I suppose no one wants Michael Jordan on his team. But here is what made Sanders stand out. He was humble. I remember tracking him down in the dressing room several times, wanting him to talk about himself. He wanted no part of it. He even refused to accept the game ball after his 2,000-yard season unless his linemen were with him.

Sanders was as spectacular as any athlete. Yet when he scored, he simply flipped the ball to the official and ran back to play another day.

Who doesn't want a guy like that on your team?

Q

As the Lions coach you are down four points with two minutes left. Which quarterback—post-Bobby Layne— do you want under center?

TERRY | Can I punt?

Sorry, I cannot take this question seriously because it's the Lions. I don't mean to be a jerk, but have the Lions had a quarterback of note since Bobby Layne was traded away in the late 1950s?

If you twist my arm, I suppose I will go with Erik Kramer. And here's why. He was rejected by the Lions until the very end during that three-headed quarterback derby with Rodney Peete and Andre Ware in the early 1990s.

And here is my philosophy about the Lions. If they make a decision, it is the wrong decision. Because the Lions rejected Kramer, I am willing to bet this was the guy who would have led the Lions to game-winning drives and maybe even the Super Bowl.

OK, I went too far. How about game-winning drives and more than one playoff win?

Kramer was functional here. He lacked a cannon arm, but he was solid and accurate, and had command of the pocket. Kramer was steady. The problem was by the time the Lions discovered this he wanted no part of the organization and bolted for Chicago. Teammates nicknamed him "Brass," because he had a larger pair of you know what than most.

After replacing an injured Peete during the last half of the 1991 season, he led the Lions to the NFC championship game. So how was he rewarded? He started just seven games the next two seasons behind Peete and sometimes behind Ware.

Kramer left the Lions for division-rival Chicago, where he enjoyed moderate success. He passed for 3,838 yards and 29 touchdowns in 1995, and I remember the joy in his eyes when he beat the Lions. He tried to play it off as another victory, but the glee in his eyes told another story.

I am willing to bet this was the guy. The Lions just didn't know it until it was too late.

DREW I think I still might take Bobby Layne—even in his current embalmed state. But since being alive is a necessary criterion, you leave me with little choice but to take Eric Hipple. Hipple just didn't give a crap about what people thought about him.

Being underappreciated was nothing new to him. He quarterbacked at little-known Utah State, because other Division I-A programs wanted nothing to do with a guy who was listed at six foot one, which was more than charitable. Hipple might have been six feet if he stood up on his toes. The Lions drafted him out of the fourth round in 1980.

As coach, I need a quarterback who loves the challenge of the moment. Terry, you know darn well there hasn't been a Lions quarterback in our lifetimes who shone brighter in one game than Hipple did on Monday night, October 19, 1981, against the Chicago Bears before a national television audience.

We have long grown accustomed to Lions quarterbacks going down during the season, fueling faith that the Next Great Hope was ready to take the next snap. But nobody expected much when then-head coach Monte Clark named Hipple the starter after Gary Danielson went down with an injury.

Now that was pressure!

Here was somebody making his first career start on *Monday Night Football*, and Hipple threw four touchdown passes, including a 94-yarder to receiver Leonard Thompson. ABC ranked Hipple's performance as one of the top 10 memories when the network celebrated the 25th anniversary of *Monday Night Football* in 1994.

The Lions devoured the Bears 48-17. Only once have the Lions scored more points in a game since—55 against those same Bears in 1997.

As coach, I need a quarterback who possesses two qualities— efficiency and stubbornness. Hipple still holds the team record for highest completion rating in a single season—62.95 percent in 1986. He'd make the right read and get the ball where it needed to go if I were trailing late in a close game. But there was also some inflexibility to Hipple. He thought a play was there even if the coaches had doubts, and that's an essential attitude when engineering a late comeback.

 # What was the most dramatic Lions touchdown?

DREW The Lions and the Cleveland Browns played three times for the NFL championship in the 1950s—and the Lions won all three times. But the most dramatic was the 1953 title game, played two days after Christmas before a snow-covered sold-out Briggs Stadium crowd of 54,577.

The Lions were the defending league champions, and the Browns had vowed revenge throughout the 1953 campaign. The Browns, at 11-1, were the top team in the Eastern Division and the 10-2 Lions were the class of the Western Division, both on a collision course for a championship rematch.

The game didn't disappoint.

The Browns took a 16-10 lead late into the fourth quarter. Confident in their defense, Cleveland punted the ball away on fourth down and short yardage inside Lions territory. They could have put the game away with a first down, taking more time off the clock.

Cleveland kicked the ball into the end zone, giving the Lions and their fearless leader, quarterback Bobby Layne, the ball at their own 20-yard line. Time turned precious, yet Layne was unfazed by the enormous odds against him at that moment. He steadily worked the Lions through the snow and down the field, spreading the ball all over the field like a conductor whirling his baton.

He completed four of six passes during that final drive, but the biggest was the last one.

Layne hit receiver Jim Doran for a 33-yard touchdown pass in the game's final seconds, giving the Lions a heart-stopping 17-16 victory over the Browns and their second straight NFL championship.

That moment remains the biggest highlight of the Lions' 72 years in Detroit. They last won an NFL championship four years later, a 59-14 blowout against those same Browns. But from a sheer standard of drama, nothing compares to the Lions' version of "The Drive" in 1953. That touchdown pass to Doran created the legend of Layne. And more than 50 years later, there hasn't been another Lions quarterback who has come remotely close to matching, let alone eclipsing, Layne's hold on the city.

TERRY | Sadly, we must go back to before my birth to talk about a dramatic Lions touchdown.

What is the one game we always talk about here in Detroit? It is the 1957 championship game. The Lions beat Cleveland 59-14 for their last championship. There were no dramatic touchdowns in this game.

But the Lions would have never gotten to that game if not for running back Gene Gedman, who only played four seasons for Detroit and was the Lions' second pick in the 1953 draft.

He led the Lions in rushing for just one season when he bulled for 479 yards and seven touchdowns in 1956.

But he came in with great credentials. There is a story of how Lions general manager Nick Kerbawy greeted two players at the bus station. He told one player how to take the bus to the Lions practice fields in Ypsilanti. Kerbawy offered to golf with Gedman before driving him to the practice site. The player Kerbawy ignored was future Hall of Fame linebacker Joe Schmidt.

A week before the championship game, the Lions trailed San Francisco 27-7 midway through the third quarter behind Niners quarterback Y.A. Tittle's three touchdown passes. The Lions were still angry over listening to the Niners celebrate at halftime through Tiger Stadium's paper-thin walls. To make matters worse, no team had ever recovered from a 20-point deficit in NFL history.

But that was about to change.

The Lions scored three touchdowns in a span of 1:47 as the defense intercepted three Tittle passes. Reserve back Thomas Tracy came off the bench to make one- and 42-yard touchdown runs.

But it was Gedman's two-yard run in the fourth quarter that put the Lions on top 28-27 and on their way to a 31-27 victory.

The turn of events stunned Niners fans, who expected their team to play Cleveland for the title. The touchdown was not as dramatic as Sterling Sharpe's game-winning touchdown *against* the Lions in the 1996 playoffs. (Remember, I was asked to do a dramatic *Lions* touchdown.)

The touchdown by Gedman represents five decades of frustration for Lions fans. It was the last time an opponent sought to hunt down the Lions. It may not have been the most dramatic touchdown in Lions history, but it causes a lot of drama with Lions fans when they reminisce about the glorious past of good football.

 **Who was the worst Lions' draft pick?**

DREW There's plenty from which to choose, but the biggest mistake ever was taking defensive end Reggie Rogers with the seventh overall selection in the 1987 draft—and it has little to do with utter lack of interest and contributions on the field. It has everything to do with that tragic evening on October 1988 when the drunken Rogers ran a red light on Pontiac Street and broadsided a car—killing three teenagers.

And he only spent a year in prison for negligent homicide.

Rogers was a disaster waiting to happen and, unfortunately, the Lions front office's apparent willingness to ignore the warning signs of questionable character screaming from his history at the University of Washington placed this waste of humanity on our streets. And three innocents paid the ultimate price.

Lions coach Darryl Rogers wanted a pass rusher, somebody who could "block out the sun" with his massive presence. The six-foot-six Rogers was an All-American at Washington but was never known for his work habits. Everything just came easy for him. There was always somebody there to excuse his sins.

Rogers was charged with drunken driving in Seattle in 1986, but a judge dropped the charge after a number of character references pleaded Rogers's virtues to the court. The argument was that he was a popular football player with a rich NFL future ahead of him, so the court should cut him some slack.

And then just weeks after the Lions chose Rogers, he was charged in Seattle with gross misdemeanor assault against a former girlfriend. He pled down to a lesser charge and got probation.

But there was a pattern that if the Lions had done their due diligence in investigating Rogers's background, they would have known that this guy was too much of a risk to chance a high first-round selection.

If there was a lesson learned from this debacle, it's that teams now hire private investigative firms to go as far back as a prospect's grammar school records to uncover anything that might be considered potentially damaging. There's too much of an investment made today, especially with the salary cap consequences for a misstep, not to know everything possible.

TERRY This is such a tough question because the Lions have made a number of first-round draft busts from Chuck Long to Andre Ware to Joey Harrington.

They were all quarterbacks. Do you see the connection? The Lions are always looking for the big quarterback score. That was why they drafted Heisman Trophy winner Andre Ware from the University of Houston in the 1990 draft. He was a fine collegiate quarterback who played well in a system. But the Lions quickly discovered he lacked touch, never could learn the offense well enough to run it, and could not beat out journeymen Rodney Peete and Erik Kramer in practice after holding out his rookie season for a better contract.

"They were all quarterbacks. Do you see the connection? The Lions are always looking for the big quarterback score."

We used to watch Ware practice, and I will give him credit—he had a cannon arm. The problem was he never knew how to throw a change up. On short pass patterns he used to bomb the chests of receivers with missiles that were too hot to handle.

Ware said Lions coach Wayne Fontes ruined his development because he handled the quarterback circus so clumsily, and he was right. (One of my favorite lines from Fontes was, "Rodney Peete is still my number-one quarterback but I am starting Andre Ware." Huh?) Fontes was under pressure from the front office to start Ware but felt uncomfortable with him.

In four seasons with the Lions he played in 14 games, passed for 1,112 yards, five touchdowns, and eight interceptions. Compare that to Ware's final season at UH where he passed for 4,699 yards and 46 touchdowns.

The Lions were supposed to build their team around Ware. Instead he left the Lions, played in the Canadian Football League where he failed again and ended his career as property of the Oakland Raiders. Coach Jon Gruden assigned him to NFL Europe's Berlin Thunder in 1999 where Ware fractured his left non-throwing shoulder and retired after five games.

# Who was the best big-play player in Lions history?

TERRY It is easy to say Barry Sanders. He is the Lions' most recognizable figure. But I am a man who loves defense, and I am going to turn to another No. 20 for this one.

No one turned games around more than former Lions defensive back and kick returner Lem Barney. Every time he touched the ball, you held your breath. Barney had speed and enough moves to make you fall out of your underwear.

We were so impressed with Barney as kids that we played a game called "Lem Barney."

We would throw a football high in the air to the kid pretending to be Lem Barney, and we'd send three or four guys after the ball carrier, who tried to elude us with his best Barney moves.

You want to talk about big plays, Barney intercepted 56 passes and returned seven of them for touchdowns.

His first pick came in the 1967 season opener when Green Bay quarterback Bart Starr tried to test the rookie by sending running back Elijah Pitts into the flat. Barney read the play, jumped on the ball, fell to the ground, and returned it 24 yards for a touchdown. Barney had 10 interceptions his rookie season and quickly earned the nickname "The Supernatural" by former Lions beat writer and columnist Jerry Green.

During his career he averaged 25.5 yards on kick returns, 19.2 yards on interception returns, and 9.2 yards on punt returns. Barney returned two punts for touchdowns and scored on a 98-yard kickoff return and 94-yard missed field goal return. Barney changed games by recovering 11 opponent fumbles and punted in 1967 and 1969.

Barney is known today for the trademark derby he wears and an outgoing personality. He is one of the nicest guys in sports and looks as if he can still play.

DREW As much as I detest giving you credit for anything, T. Fost, I admire the fact that you didn't opt for the clichéd "Barry Sanders is God" argument for everything Honolulu blue and silver. Lem Barney lorded over Detroit during his playing career through on-field and off-field dynamism, but there has been only one Detroit Lion in the franchise's 72 years in the Motor City who truly revolutionized the game.

The man they called Night Train.

Dick "Night Train" Lane took out the anger of his abandonment at three months old in Austin, Texas, against those who dared catch a pass across the middle of the field. He was the NFL's first physically aggressive defensive back when he joined the Los Angeles Rams in 1952. At six feet, three inches and 185 pounds, Lane was bigger than the average receiver. He'd grab his intended victims around the neck and horse-collar them to the ground.

> "[Dick] Lane was the game's first defensive 'headhunter,' bringing a viciousness and physicial brutality to the game..."

Guys that size were usually linebackers, but Night Train possessed such unusual speed that he was used primarily at defensive back.

Lane was the game's first defensive "headhunter," bringing a viciousness and physical brutality to the game that made the NFL stand out in the 1950s as the sport gradually morphed into the national mainstream.

The tackle was called "The Night Train Necktie."

The NFL eventually banned the tackle.

When Lane came to the Lions in 1960, he was still regarded as one of the game's top defensive backs. He earned three Pro Bowl appearances in his six years in Detroit.

He didn't just make the big play, but Night Train was a big player as well. Married to famed blues singer Dinah Washington, the Lanes were a big celebrity couple in Detroit, regularly frequenting the top nightclubs in Detroit, incorporating a degree of outward style that Detroit really hadn't seen before with its star athletes.

Lane is the only Lion to earn a spot on the NFL's 75th diamond anniversary all-league team.

HARDWOOD
HEAD TO HEAD

Who was the better Pistons coach— Chuck Daly or Larry Brown?

DREW | I'm new school in this case.
It's L.B.

Look beyond all of his idiosyncrasies and the nastiness of his departure. Concentrate on his achievements, and it's not even a close race. In two years, Brown led the Pistons to two NBA Finals—one championship and the other just one quarter away from a second title.

The Bad Boys had more talent. Chuck Daly had Isiah, an unquestioned first-ballot Hall of Famer, as his starting point.

All L.B. had was his reputation.

Spare me the spew about Larry inheriting the best defensive player in the game in Ben Wallace and two up-and-coming offensive stars in Chauncey Billups and Rip Hamilton!

And it's convenient to lament that Larry merely finished the job that Rick Carlisle started with consecutive 50-win seasons and a trip to the Eastern Conference finals. Carlisle may have given the team its start, but Brown created the championship blueprint.

Also, Chuck already had a point guard, Brown had to build one.

A championship team assumes the character of its strongest personality. It was Isiah with the Bad Boys, but it was Larry with the 2004 champions.

It wasn't long into Larry's first season with the Pistons before he gnawed on Billups's nerves, frequently calling out the point guard in

Did Larry Brown's status as the new man in town supplant the legacy of Chuck Daly?

front of teammates for mistakes in running the offense. Before Larry could build the point guard he wanted in Billups, he had to tear down the shooting guard he inherited.

Larry knew there would be a process in accomplishing this task. Billups would have to be broken down by going through different phases of embarrassment, anger, and stubbornness. But the coach knew that eventually Billups would break down and accept Brown's way of thinking—because it was the coach with the Hall of Fame résumé, not the player.

Who can argue with the results? It worked, didn't it?

T E R R Y | What's the difference between Chuck Daly and Larry Brown? Daly sticks around for the end of a fight; Brown runs for the next courtship.

Brown is the master of Xs and Os. He's a teacher and gym rat. And he might be the best coach in the NBA.

Daly never got credit for being a master technician. He was never named NBA Coach of the Year.

But Daly's strength was understanding each player's personality and needs. He always said that he didn't have 12 players but rather 12 separate corporations. The expression "a player's coach" was coined with Daly in mind.

Chuck was the master of working with people. He realized that different players responded to different motivational techniques. Daly's assistants often shared with the beat writers a description of the coach's style—when he got mad at Isiah Thomas, he yelled at John Salley.

Isiah didn't respond to direct confrontation and was better handled with coddling. But Salley often was reached only through yelling.

Daly worked on the mind. He made players think they were pushing the buttons, when, in fact, Daly was devising the master plan.

For example, the coach would suggest something he knew would work, but he allowed protesting players to try own their way.

Did Chuck Daly do enough with the Bad Boys to be the top Pistons coach?

Eventually those players saw things Daly's way and would bring up one of his ideas to him. Daly's eyes would light up, and he'd scream, "Great idea!"

It was Daly's deal, but the players thought they were shuffling the cards.

Let's go back to Game 1 of the 1990 NBA Finals for an example. Daly called a late timeout with the game tied against Portland.

He drew up a play called "One-C," which called for Thomas to take the ball off the high post, get a screen from Laimbeer, read the defensive adjustment, and either drive to the basket, attempt a pull-up jumper, or give Laimbeer a late feed at the three-point arc.

But all Daly said in that huddle was that he didn't want Portland to have any chance at a miracle last shot. He knew Thomas would take control of the situation. And Thomas did, telling everyone that he was keeping the ball on his play. Either Zeek would sink the shot at the buzzer and the Pistons would win, or there would be overtime.

It looked like Thomas ran the huddle, but it was Daly who got the play he wanted in that situation.

Who was the most important Pistons' first-round draft pick?

TERRY | Isiah Thomas developed the blueprint that Dumars enacted when he became team president.

When Dumars talked about getting back to a "Pistons attitude," he was reminiscing about the tone once set by Zeke.

Those of us covering the team used to joke about Thomas running the team, but that wasn't far from the truth. He did more than just shoot the ball and pass to open teammates. Thomas established the Bad Boys. It was a product of his childhood in the Chicago projects, where strength was measured by the lengths to which a young man would go to avoid falling into the wrong crowd.

The Pistons captain would ask his teammates, "How far are you willing to push yourself to be a champion?" And he expected his teammates to push themselves to the limit—and then some.

Isiah created and enforced the rules that to this day remain at The Palace.

Do you see much of a difference between Rick Mahorn and Ben Wallace or Dennis Rodman and Tayshaun Prince? They're similar players. Dumars saw much of Mahorn in Wallace and much of Rodman in Prince. He's borrowing from what Thomas built.

Thomas, generally considered one of the top 10 to ever play in the NBA, never backed down from a fight, regardless of the opponent's size. In 1990, he took on seven-footer Bill Cartwright in the hostile environment of Chicago Stadium after Cartwright delivered what

Thomas thought was a cheap shot to the head on a pick-and-roll. Those in the crowd and on press row chuckled at the image of a six-foot flea challenging a mountain. But players knew better. Forget the angelic smile and his mother Mary's innocent sighs, "Oh, Isiah," in TV and radio commercials. You didn't get Isiah Thomas mad. If need be, the captain would fight until the last breath to win, and his no-nonsense attitude rubbed off on his teammates.

That determination stuck with Dumars, and he rebuilt it in the current team.

D R E W | You're such an Isiah "slappie."

Zeke was—and may forever be—the most talented player ever to wear a Pistons jersey, but Joe Dumars has made the most important and most enduring imprint on this franchise.

Thomas has two NBA championships. Dumars has three.

This is a bottom-line business, and Dumars has become this NBA generation's Jerry West—smooth yet deadly as a championship player and coldly calculating as a championship chief executive.

If Thomas hadn't joined the team in 1981, there wouldn't have been a first championship. But if Dumars hadn't followed four years later, not only wouldn't there have been a first NBA title, but there wouldn't have been a championship revival 14 years later as well.

Let's be brutally honest, how many people actually believed that Dumars possessed a clue of how to run the organization when he became team president in June 2000? Was he named president merely because he was a familiar face? Was he little more than a popular link to the past?

It's ironic that Dumars learned plenty from Thomas's aborted power play to move upstairs into the Pistons' executive suite immediately following Thomas's retirement from the Pistons. Thomas thought he had a deal with owner Bill Davidson, but the then-historic transition was purportedly undermined through news leaks that painted Thomas's intentions in a negative light.

Once Dumars's playing days ended in 1999, he took a year off. Dumars thought he could better gain the players' trust as their new boss if there was a suitable adjustment period for them to no longer view him as a former teammate.

Since then, Dumars has devised the outline for building a championship team without the need of a maximum contract superstar or "max out" player, a plan soon to be replicated with other organizations.

Consider the overall body of work.

In 20 years as a Piston, Dumars has an NBA Finals' Most Valuable Player award, three NBA championship rings—two as a player and one as its chief executive, and the NBA's annual citizenship award renamed in his honor.

 # Who is the best Pistons sidekick?

TERRY | "Leon The Barber" was my guy.

I love it when a blue-collar guy from Detroit's gritty near-west side can make millionaire basketball players cringe.

Many players were clipped by The Barber.

Leon stood in front of his seat unleashing barrages of profanity and witty one-liners. Most NBA players simply took it in stride. Others tried to fire back. But that only made Leon more vicious, and the players backed off.

The Barber became a Motor City institution.

He was at the front of a new wave in the NBA in the 1970s—the colorfully vocal fans who aren't afraid to draw attention to themselves.

Leon initially sat behind the Pistons' bench when they played at Cobo Arena in downtown Detroit. The Pistons were primarily basement dwellers then, and Leon openly vented his frustrations to the team—even to All-Stars such as Bob Lanier.

The coaches and players finally had enough of his insults. So the Pistons organization came up with the then-revolutionary idea of putting Leon's seat behind the visitors' bench. The team didn't want to change his act; they just wanted Leon to have a different audience—and effect.

But there was a compassionate side to Leon, too. He helped kids in a Detroit youth center. He went there nearly every day to teach kids the importance of staying in school and out of trouble.

Players ultimately befriended him. You wanted The Barber as a friend and not a foe.

When Leon died, Lanier attended his funeral.

DREW | It's the "go-to-it" guy, Mike Abdenour. Abdenour came to the Pistons as its trainer and morphed into a much-adored unofficial team mascot.

There isn't a non-player or coach who's more identified with the last two decades of this franchise's history than Abdenour.

His role has extended beyond the functions of wrapping up sprains.

Chuck Daly employed him as a sentry during timeouts, scoping out the opposing huddle, alerting the coaches about the next substitutions.

But Daly found the best use for Abdenour's grating shrill.

Whenever the 24-second shot clock hit five seconds, it was Abdenour's job to leap off the bench and sound the offensive alarm—"Go to it! Go to it!"

Get a shot off—quickly!

Isiah Thomas once joked to me that they could be playing before a boisterously packed Boston Garden in Game 7 of the Eastern Conference finals, and they could still decipher Abdenour's instructions from the din.

> **"There isn't a non-player or coach who's more identified with the last two decades of this franchise's history than [Mike] Abdenour."**

Abdenour got swept up in the game to the ire of opposing coaches and many referees, but there was never any questioning his passion or loyalty.

Perhaps the biggest compliment he ever received was when a reporter asked Daly about the difficult transition of a college coach going directly to the NBA as a head coach. Daly said that his trainer had more expertise in managing the flow of an NBA game from the bench than a college head coach.

Abdenour made the jump to the big leagues from Wayne State University in Detroit in 1975. At the end of the 2005-2006 season, he will have finished his 30th year in the NBA—and 27th with the Pistons.

He left the Pistons briefly after the 1992 season, following Daly's exit. But Abdenour couldn't stay away long, returning three years later—because he's all about Detroit.

 **The Pistons scheduled a press conference for Isiah Thomas to make him a Piston for life, but it never happened. Why?**

TERRY Pistons owner Bill Davidson and Thomas reached an agreement where he agreed to pay Thomas $17 million and give him a small percentage of the team for helping turn the Pistons into an elite franchise.

This was a sensitive deal, and Davidson did not want word to leak to the public. Thomas, in his glee, told relatives, and they in turn told some of their buddies in the Chicago media. The story leaked, and Davidson felt betrayed and embarrassed. More importantly, he felt he could not trust Thomas.

The secondary issue is the stormy relationship between Palace and Entertainment CEO Tom Wilson and Thomas. Both wanted control of the team. And both were instrumental in making Davidson a lot of money.

Thomas was crushed in the power struggle as Wilson demonstrated his value to the franchise over the long term with his superior marketing skills.

We knew Wilson would do his job well. Would Thomas have made a great front office executive? We joked that Thomas acted as general manager during his 13-year playing career with the Pistons. But moving him from the floor to run a team was a risk Davidson did not want to take.

Wilson was the better choice, so Davidson banished Thomas from the kingdom.

"I would say [the relationship] is friendly and respectful," Thomas said. "But as far as ever working for the Pistons, that ship left the dock a long time ago. I am happy with my place in basketball. I didn't have a choice but to put it behind me. There was no opportunity for me here, and at the same time it was made very clear there was no opportunity for me here. You wake up. You go out and go find a job."

Davidson also heard rumors of Thomas's involvement in "high-stakes gambling" and did not want that infiltrating his franchise. Thomas is a risk taker who goes for the home run every time he steps to the plate. Davidson wanted to go the safe route.

D R E W | There was prejudice involved here—and, no, I'm not talking about racial prejudice, so everybody just take a deep breath and chill. There was a prejudice against players moving immediately from the court to the front office without any prior experience. There's basketball and there's business, and owners always separated the two. They've loved and respected the brilliance players exhibited on the floor. They trusted them running the show from the floor, but it was something else altogether running the show from the boardroom.

The game itself was the owners' toy, but the business of running that game was their primary interest. And they want businessmen in charge, not basketball players.

Thomas courageously tried changing the rules. His mistakes helped open the doors for former star players like Larry Bird, Michael Jordan, and Joe Dumars in later years when they ascended to the executive throne.

A little patience would have taken Thomas a long way, as well as a little less sense of entitlement. Had he earned the opportunity to move into the front office and run the Pistons? Absolutely. But he should have taken a year or two away from the game and distanced himself from Isiah Thomas the player, getting everybody slowly acclimated to his new role of Isiah Thomas the chief executive. He had developed other business interests such as some printing company franchises in the final years of his career with the Pistons. He needed to beef up his business credentials. But he thought of himself as lord of the manor, considering the special relationship he had with Pistons owner Bill Davidson. But the only loyalty in business is the faithfulness of keeping the operation in the black fiscally. That's why Davidson opted for Palace president Tom Wilson to run the Pistons as well instead of Thomas. It proved a colossal disaster. But Davidson learned the error of his ways, opting for Dumars once Dumars's playing days were done. But Dumars learned as well and slowly made the transition from team player to team president.

Perhaps that's part of Thomas's legacy as well.

# Could Tom Izzo coach an NBA team to the world championship?

DREW It won't happen, because when college coaches, even the best of them, make the jump to the NBA, it's often a leap into the garbage. Even when Mike Krzyzewski flirted with going to the Los Angeles Lakers, he wasn't getting a crack at a championship contender, but a team that was headed on the downward slope.

Izzo should go the NBA eventually and fund his retirement. I've told him on a number of occasions that the NBA is a purer form of coaching than college basketball. If you're running an elite college program, you're spending as much time recruiting to replace 19-year-old prima donnas who are confident that they're draft lottery picks, but are destined to ride the bus along the minor league prairie circuit than you are teaching players in practice. You have to deal with spoiled alumni who can't understand that you can't get to the Final Four every year.

"[Tom Izzo is] much better prepared emotionally now for the challenges of meshing his personality with those of the millionaires he'd coach."

In the NBA, he doesn't have a hypocritical governing body, the NCAA, holding the coach accountable for everything his players do away from the court, yet it drastically limits the amount of contact the coach can have with the player. All he must worry about is 82 games and not getting overly emotional if things aren't exactly following the script after the 20th game.

But for Izzo to win an NBA championship, he would have to join either an established contender or an up-and-coming team like the Cleveland Cavaliers who possess a young megastar like LeBron James. And no front-office executive would entrust such responsibility to a college coach.

Izzo worked with former Pistons coach Larry Brown, watching practices and learning the nuances of the basic offensive and defensive schemes. He's much better prepared emotionally now for the challenges of meshing his personality with those of the millionaires he'd coach.

But all of that means diddly unless there's a solid infrastructure already in place, and nobody will be willing to give Izzo the keys to the car, unless ownership doesn't really care if the car can't go forward.

TERRY Many people don't know that Tom Izzo received a crash course on the NBA from former Pistons coach Larry Brown during the 2004 Pistons NBA championship drive.

Izzo and his buddy Marquette coach Tom Crean sat in on Pistons' staff meetings to see the innerworkings of a championship coaching staff. They studied offensive and defensive strategy. They watched game film and detailed breakdowns on Pistons' opponents. They know how to prepare for Shaquille O'Neal, Kobe Bryant, Allen Iverson, and Michael Redd.

But mostly Izzo learned how to deal with people.

A few years ago I was the first in line saying Izzo lacked enough people skills to run an NBA team. I was a primary voice discouraging

Izzo from taking the Atlanta Hawks job after he won the 2000 national championship. It was a bad mix.

Izzo did not understand how to soothe delicate NBA egos, and the Hawks remain one of the worst franchises in team history. Illinois coach Lon Kruger took the job and lasted less than three seasons.

Izzo is a passionate man. That passion helped lead Michigan State to four Final Fours. The Spartans remain an elite program, because Izzo's fire lit a fuse.

In college he can get away with using shoulder pads in practice. He can grab guys and scream in their faces. He cannot do that in the NBA.

Izzo did not understand that at first. Now he does, thanks to Larry Brown.

Izzo learned to pace himself. You do not win a title in one day. He is a brilliant basketball mind. Over the years he's coached running teams, half-court teams, tough teams, and soft teams—often in the same season.

In 2000 he pounded it out during the Big Ten season with Wisconsin and then ran past Florida in the championship game. That's the right guy for any job.

Q There's one opening on the Pistons' all-time starting lineup, which already includes Isiah Thomas and Dave Bing in the backcourt, Bob Lanier at center, and Dennis Rodman as one forward. Who do you pick to fill the last slot?

TERRY Pistons general manager Billy McKinney broke down in tears when he selected Grant Hill with the third selection overall in the 1994 NBA draft. The director of player personnel thought he found a savior.

Hill was a marketing director's dream. A four-year star at Duke University, Hill was equally comfortable playing Mozart on the piano as he was playing small forward.

Grant, who averaged 21.6 points, 7.8 rebounds, and 6.3 assists, was anointed the rightful heir to Michael Jordan's legacy immediately. He was voted onto the All-Star Game's starting lineup for his first five years in the league. Hill was smooth off the dribble and an excellent defender. He introduced the point-forward position to the Pistons.

It wasn't his fault that mismanagement surrounded him with clowns, misfits, and malcontents. And his accomplishments, including leading the team in scoring in each of his six seasons in Detroit, shouldn't carry the taint of him bolting from the team through free agency in the summer of 2000.

The dude had a hard edge to his game. The problem is the public views him as soft.

Now, Drew, you know I love you like a brother. But "Bad News" Barnes? This is not the Pistons all-jerk team. We are trying to include people who wanted to play here and tried to win.

Hill wanted to lift the franchise to great heights. Bad News wanted to promote Bad News. And he did a great job of it.

Hill did not work out here. In fact, the best thing to happen to the Pistons was the sign and trade with Orlando that sent Hill to the Magic for Ben Wallace and Chucky Atkins. It provided the building block for the Pistons' championship-caliber teams.

By then Hill was broken down with a chronic foot injury that has limited his play and turned him into a more passive player. He gave his health to the franchise, and we should recognize that.

Besides, if he couldn't play, no one would have signed him to a contract. There is no way you could put Barnes and his attitude on the open market and work a similar sign and trade.

D R E W   This won't be a popular selection. It's just the right one. Marvin "Bad News" Barnes was the most talented forward ever to play in Detroit, and that's the primary characteristic from which to judge an all-time team. I concede that the man even gave cancer a bad name. ESPN once ranked him as one of the top five disruptive personalities in NBA history.

But the boy had skills. He had a lot of other things as well—issues that today would have made him a regular fixture on *SportsCenter* or maybe Court TV. He once clubbed a teammate at Providence with a tire iron. Barnes didn't just carry around emotional baggage. He had a full set of luggage.

But he started the parade of big athletic forwards who were equally successful facing the basket and putting the ball on the floor as they were on the low block with their backs to the basket. He created tremendous matchup problems, because the NBA wasn't accustomed to having six-foot-nine players run the floor as fluidly as Barnes.

Did he waste his immense gift? Absolutely.

But it's the gift that we're honoring with this team.

Barnes is the answer to an infamous local trivia question. The Pistons bypassed Moses Malone in the 1976 ABA dispersal draft to draft whom? Barnes only played 68 games as a Piston, before his corrosive personality as well as drug and alcohol problems drove him out of town and soon afterwards, the league.

During an HBO interview in 2005, Barnes spoke of how he came to the arena on game nights with two fully loaded revolvers. He'd hang them up on the rack in his locker room cubicle and nobody ever said anything to him about it.

Could you blame them? The man was packing serious heat! There could have been a misunderstanding. That's why people buy guns in the first place. Too many misunderstandings!

Barnes also admitted to doing cocaine while on the bench in Boston during his last season in 1979. He was but one of the reasons why the NBA wasn't considered a mainstream professional sport in the days before Magic Johnson and Larry Bird came to the rescue.

Unfortunately, he lived up to his nickname. But there wasn't a more talented forward in a Pistons uniform.

Who would have won a best-of-seven series between the 1989 and the 2004 Pistons?

DREW | Let's give the 2004 fellas their props. They might be the best championship story in recent Detroit sports history if only because they were the city's first championship underdog.

Yet, the Bad Boys still rule!

If you remove from the equation the Hall of Fame backcourt of Isiah Thomas and Joe Dumars, even the second team—James Edwards; John Salley; Dennis Rodman; Vinnie Johnson; and "The Human 10-Day Contract," Gerald Henderson—would have pushed the 2004 Pistons seriously.

What matchup does the 2004 team win?

Rasheed Wallace gets the nod over Bill Laimbeer because of his inside-outside capabilities.

And you might take Tayshaun Prince over Mark Aguirre because of his defensive strengths.

But Ben Wallace and Rick Mahorn are a draw. Big Ben is a tremendous weak-side defender and embodies the 2004 team's spirit. But Mahorn *was* the Bad Boys.

My enduring image of Mahorn is a mental snapshot of the devilish forward in the 1989 Finals. He was shoving a hand in James Worthy's face as the Laker went up for a shot. Nothing scurrilous about that—until you glance a little lower to see Mahorn's left hand grabbing just enough of the waistband of Worthy's trunks to hinder his elevation.

That was Pistons poetry back in the day.

The 1989 team was one of the best championship teams in NBA history, a pedigree honed from their cold-blooded attitude. The Bad Boys weren't just satisfied with victory. They wanted your heart in their grasp, squeezing away every last drop of the opponent's will. Then, they'd do a victory jig on it for good measure.

The 1989 team swept the Lakers in four games.

And afterward in a champagne-sweaty locker room, NBA commissioner David Stern presented Thomas with the Larry O'Brien Trophy. Eyes filled with tears, Thomas not only kissed it—he practically made love to it.

His tears in 1989 were of a different tone from the previous year after a tough Game 7 loss to the Lakers at the Forum. Thomas, unable to contribute anything in that game because of a severely sprained ankle incurred in Game 6, wouldn't leave the shower. He sat there and cried. But it planted a seed. Zeke often said that few things hurt him more than losing, and that's what made the 1989 championship all the more fulfilling.

Thomas shattered the myth that a little guy couldn't become the centerpiece of a world championship team. That was his goal.

In this dream matchup of the 1989 versus 2004 Pistons, I'll take the Bad Boys in six games.

TERRY | Finally, we agree on something. The 1989 Pistons would win this series.

The 1989 team was deeper and tougher, and played in an era with more dangerous teams.

The Bad Boys wore teams out with superior depth and intimidation. So the 2004 team could win this potential matchup only if it took the first two games and hung on.

Let's compare benches.

The 1989 Pistons had a bench that would have started for most teams in the NBA—Vinnie Johnson, Mark Aguirre, James Edwards, and John Salley.

Isiah Thomas would often tell the beat writers that the toughest games were on the practice floor sometimes because the second unit took so much pride in beating the starters. Chuck Daly knew that such strong competition would make everybody tougher on game nights. And it did.

Johnson was the called "The Microwave" for a reason. He heated up quickly, changing the offensive tempo when he entered the game. Edwards was the conductor of "the Buddah train," named for the Pistons' propensity to ride the Fu-Manchued One's low-post offensive game for extended periods. We sometimes mocked the lanky Salley for taking weeks off at a time during the regular season, but he was difficult to score on because of his long wingspan and leaping ability.

The 2004 Pistons bench was hardly frightening. Mehmet Okur, Lindsey Hunter, Mike James, and Elden Campbell were acceptable components, but that team was more about its starting five. The 1989 Bad Boys were about the entire team.

But the main reason the 2004 Pistons could not win is because of expansion. There were six fewer teams in 1989, so the talent was more concentrated. Imagine dropping a guy like Cleveland Cavaliers forward Drew Gooden or Memphis Grizzlies forward Shane Battier on the 2004 Pistons. That would be an interesting bench. The 1989 Pistons starting frontcourt of Bill Laimbeer, Rick Mahorn, and Dennis Rodman would hold its own against 2004 starters Rasheed Wallace, Tayshaun Prince, and Ben Wallace. Rodman and Ben Wallace became the symbols for their respective team's defensive personalities. But you could stick Rodman on anybody one on one, even an opposing center, and "The Worm" could contain him. Ben Wallace was a better "help defender" in that his quickness was better used leaving his man away from the ball and running at the shooter on the other side of the floor. It requires remarkable athleticism, but it's easier than what was asked of Rodman—lock up your guy without needing assistance from a teammate.

I'll take the Bad Boys in six.

Are the Bad Boys, led by Isiah Thomas, good enough to send Ben Wallace and his crew packing?

SKATING AROUND THE SUBJECT

Who is the face of the Red Wings— Steve Yzerman or Gordie Howe?

DREW Steve Yzerman or Gordie Howe: That's nearly an impossible choice to make. But Yzerman's missing-tooth grin as he holds up the Stanley Cup in 1997 after a 42-year Detroit absence is the enduring image of this franchise.

Yzerman stands out just a smidgeon further than Howe because of what he was asked to do to elevate the Wings into a perennial Stanley Cup championship contender.

Yzerman was a pure scorer, well on his way to surpassing Howe's then–NHL career record of 801 goals. Yzerman had 445 goals after his 10th season in 1993.

When coach Scotty Bowman arrived in 1993, the first person he spoke with was his young captain. Bowman saw a team too reliant on outscoring its opposition. He demanded sacrifice, and it had to start with Yzerman. The coach wanted less scoring and more defense from him.

Change came grudgingly. Asking someone who averaged 40-plus goals a season to care more about dropping to the ice to block a shot on the penalty kill isn't an easy sell. But Bowman knew that if he could convince Yzerman, everyone else would fall in line.

Beginning with the 1994-1995 season, Yzerman never scored more than 36 goals in any season. But that season began a 10-year run in which the Wings won three Stanley Cups and additional Presidents

Trophies (four), which are awarded for the best regular-season record. The Wings also won more playoff games (91) than any other NHL team.

The cartilage in Yzerman's knees abandoned him long before his desire to play the game. In summer 2002, it drove him to have an osteotomy, a surgical procedure in which the knee joints are shaved to reduce friction. It was the first time a NHL player opted for such an operation, and Yzerman's successful return to the ice suggests that the procedure might become a more viable option for players. Just one more chapter added to the legacy.

TERRY When Gordie Howe was a teenager, he knew he was destined for greatness. He used to practice signing his autograph on blank sheets of paper.

It proved prophetic. Howe had a 25-year career with the Wings that produced franchise records in goals (786), assists (1,023), points (1,850), and games played (1,687)—numbers that to this day rank second overall in NHL history.

Howe could score, defend, skate, and pound his opponents into the next county.

In today's game, a player of Howe's pedigree would be protected. Opponents wouldn't dare touch him, and his teammates would place a protective shield around him.

> "Howe could score, defend, skate, and pound his opponents into the next county."

But Howe wanted none of that. He fought his own battles.

What makes his feat more amazing is that he played much of his career without a curved stick, which puts more speed and accuracy on a slap shot.

Howe won four Stanley Cups when the NHL was a six-team league. The talent was not as diluted as it has been during Yzerman's era. And during Howe's day, the Canadian-dominated NHL did everything it could to ensure the Montreal Canadiens and Toronto Maple Leafs ruled the ice.

Howe taught guys grit and determination through actions. A telling career statistic is that Howe is the Wings career leader in game-winning goals: 121. That speaks volumes about a player's reliability when the pressure is highest. And after he'd score the winning goal, he'd give his defender an elbow to the chops for good measure.

Yzerman is a fine and solid modern-day player, but Howe's career transcends time.

Can a hockey legend (a.k.a. Gordie Howe [right]) outscore Steve Yzerman as the representative of the Red Wings?

# The Wings have won three Stanley Cups in 10 years. Why?

DREW | Money is important, but it's more important to invest it wisely. When Mike Ilitch bought the Wings in 1982, Jimmy Devellano was his first hire. Plucked from the three-time defending Stanley Cup champion New York Islander's front office, Devellano was entrusted in restoring the once-proud Red Wings franchise back to respectability.

The Wings were his first position as a general manager. But Devellano's strong scouting background taught him that shrewd drafting and patient development were key to long-term success. When Devellano achieved his goal of bringing the Stanley Cup back home to Detroit in 1997 for the first time in 42 years, nine of the 17 players dressed for that series-clinching victory against Philadelphia were Devellano draft choices.

But Jimmy D's true genius was recognizing that the NHL had long ignored scouting European talent. Devellano sold Ilitch on the importance of having a full-time scouting operation overseas in 1984.

Devellano's early foreign efforts didn't yield much success. But then came the 1989 entry draft.

The Wings selected Swedish defenseman Nicklas Lidstrom in the third round, flashy Soviet skater Sergei Fedorov in the fourth round, and rugged Russian defenseman Vladimir Konstantinov in the 11th round.

All three became irreplaceable pieces of the 1997 Stanley Cup championship run.

Today, every NHL team has a full-time European scouting department.

How much does Ilitch think of Devellano?

Every time he announces another new change in direction for his Detroit Tigers, Ilitch speaks of finding "his Jimmy Devellano" for his baseball team.

TERRY Sure, front office guys Jimmy Devellano and Ken Holland invested the money wisely, but if Mike Ilitch doesn't give them the credit card, no acquisitions are made. To trace the roots of success, follow the money.

The Wings were already loaded with star talent and a huge payroll in the summer of 2001. But they were three years removed from their last Stanley Cup. So Ilitch threw more money at the problem, plucking three Hall of Fame players in a matter of days. They traded for goalie Dominik Hasek, who was making $8 million a year. That's a bone that would have choked most owners, but Ilitch understood that if he wanted to win, he had to pay. Ilitch also signed aging free-agent forwards Brett Hull and Luc Robitaille to contracts that rolled eyes elsewhere in the NHL.

Because of those acquisitions, the Wings rolled to a 116-point season and won the 2002 Stanley Cup.

This was no front office genius. If the Wings needed something, they bought it. The Wings took advantage of the financially disabled, similar to the New York Yankees.

Teams that tried beating Ilitch at his own game lost.

Carolina Hurricanes owner Peter Karmanos thought he found Ilitch's limit in 1998 when he signed Wings' restricted free agent Sergei Fedorov to a six-year, $36 million offer that required an upfront signing bonus of $26 million. The Wings protested the contract, but an arbitrator ruled the offer valid.

So what did Ilitch do? He cut the check to keep Fedorov.

 Terry Sawchuk is the best Wings goalie ever. But if there was a Game 7 of the Stanley Cup finals, which other Wings goalie do you want in net?

DREW The Wings trusted Dominik Hasek, but they would have gone to war for Mike Vernon. And that's why you'd want him between the pipes in a winner-take-all seventh game of the Finals.

The Wings determined after another embarrassing first-round exit from the 1994 Stanley Cup playoffs that they needed championship-hardened nerves in net for the following season. So they traded popular defenseman Steve Chiasson to Calgary for the veteran Vernon who was in net when the Flames won the Stanley Cup in 1989.

Vernon was hailed as the savior, carrying the Wings to the Stanley Cup Finals in 1995 for the first time in 30 years. But the New Jersey Devils swept the Wings, and just that quickly, Vernon was branded a catastrophe in pads along the likes of vilified predecessors like Tim Cheveldae.

But then came the evening of March 26, 1997—Wings versus Colorado.

Immediately after the opening faceoff, the Wings' Darren McCarty targeted the Avalanches' Claude Lemieux and exacted his pound of flesh for Lemieux's smashing the Wings' Kris Draper's face into the boards the previous year in the playoffs.

But then Vernon called out Colorado's bombastic goalie, Patrick Roy, daring Roy to face him at center ice.

The two went at it. The Joe Louis Arena crowd went wild. And Vernon's teammates found their cohesive spirit.

From that point on, Vernon was their guy. It didn't matter that Chris Osgood was considered the Wings' No. 1 goalie at the time. Coach Scotty Bowman always correlated the playoffs to a foxhole. Who do you want in there with you?

He chose Vernon.

The players knew after the fight that Vernon had their backs, so they made sure they had his. You desperately need that camaraderie in a Game 7.

Vernon was magnificent in the 1997 playoffs, going 16-4 with one shutout and goals against average of 1.76 per game. He was voted the Conn Smythe Award, representative of the most valuable player of the Stanley Cup playoffs.

And when the final seconds ticked down in Game 4 against Philadelphia in the finals at Joe Louis Arena, Vernon pulled a victory cigar out of his glove. He had slipped it in there during the last timeout a minute earlier.

TERRY You picked Mike Vernon over Dominik Hasek? That's like picking Oprah Winfrey over Tyra Banks in a beauty contest simply because Oprah doesn't talk as much.

Hasek was quirky to say the least. When he was with the Buffalo Sabres, he once flushed a teammate's suit down the toilet because other teammates teased Hasek because his clothes made him look like the Kramer character on *Seinfeld*.

Hasek had little tolerance for mindless levity. Who cares about a guy's clothes? He thought that sapped concentration from what really mattered—winning. And isn't that the attitude you want if the job is to win one big game?

You want someone who appreciates pressure. There's nothing more nerve-wracking than carrying the weight of your countrymen squarely on your shoulders. Hasek did that at the 1998 Winter Olympics in Nagano, Japan, in the gold medal hockey game between his native Czech Republic and Canada.

The gold medal came down to a sudden-death shootout. It was mano-a-mano—Hasek versus an opposing scorer.

And Hasek stoned him, stopping the shot and becoming a national hero.

Most people will tell you that the second-best goalie in NHL history, behind Patrick Roy, is Hasek. The rest will tell you Hasek is the best goalie to ever strap on pads.

The Wings needed one piece to win a Stanley Cup in 2001-2002. They willingly gave up Slava Kozlov and a first-round pick for Hasek, and they won the Cup with him leading the way.

You talk about one game? How about Hasek's NHL-record six playoff shutouts in 2002?

Hasek stopped 17 shots in the Cup-clinching game in Carolina and stopped the Hurricanes' Erik Cole on a breakaway in a Wings 3-0 victory. Of course, the series was over before that because Hasek did not allow a goal the final 127 minutes of the Cup finals.

He's called "The Dominator." They call Vernon "The Five-Hole Kid." That should be the end of the discussion right there.

Could a second NHL team survive in Detroit?

DREW A second baseball, football, or basketball team couldn't survive here, but a second hockey team could. The hardcore hockey fan base in the Detroit area is stronger here than in any other major metropolitan area. Many people in Michigan deeply love the sport, not just the Red Wings.

Three years before Mike Ilitch purchased the Wings in 1982, he founded the Little Caesars Amateur Hockey League. When it began, there were 30 teams and 450 players. But it has grown to 900 teams and more than 16,000 players, becoming the largest youth hockey league in the United States.

That's a market worth tapping.

Hockey isn't a cheap sport with purchasing equipment and renting ice time. But hockey-crazed families make the investment to play the sport, and they would make the same commitment to buying tickets if a second NHL team played in the Detroit area.

Hockey's revenue is generated primarily through ticket sales. It doesn't lean on television rights fees like other sports. And there are plenty of people on the Red Wings' season-ticket waiting list, and they've been there for years, waiting for the opportunity to be game regulars.

You're telling me they wouldn't jump at the opportunity to get season tickets for another NHL team in the area?

People love the Red Wings, but they love hockey more!

There was prior speculation that Compuware owner Peter Karmanos might move his Hartford Whalers team to the Palace of Auburn Hills. The Red Wings threatened legal action, saying that they have territorial rights to the area.

Karmanos eventually moved his team to Raleigh, North Carolina, after taxpayers agreed to build the team an arena.

The Wings simply didn't want the competition.

TERRY | We've been blinded by the Red Wings marketing ploy of calling this "Hockeytown." I love the "Hey! Hey! Hockeytown!" music videos. I think Karen Newman, who sings the national anthem at the games, is cute. And the purple octopus has become a popular kid's toy.

But this is a football and baseball town.

There's an old joke that there are 20,000 hockey fans in a city, and they all show up at each game. There are a few more passionate fans here in part because we are so close to Canada. But the number of fans in the area needs to be tripled to support a second team.

Drew, your argument that the popularity of amateur hockey shows that this city would support a second team is silly. There are more amateur soccer leagues in metro Detroit than anything else, but if you brought a professional soccer team here, you would not fill Wayne State Stadium.

The NHL returned this season after an 18-month layoff, and there has not been much buzz in Hockeytown. I understand the game being hurt in other cities like Dallas and Phoenix. But Detroit?

People wait until the playoffs until getting excited about the Wings.

It is very difficult to get Red Wings talk going during the regular season on my show *The Sports Inferno*. But you can talk Lions 24/7/365.

So you think another NHL team could work here? OK. Where do you put a second arena? Would it be in northern Oakland County, out of the reach of Canadian fans? Or would it go downriver, where incomes are not high enough to support the venture?

A second arena wouldn't be welcomed downtown: Red Wings owner Mike Ilitch would fight to protect his interests, as he has before. And he deserves that.

Could a franchise survive at The Palace of Auburn Hills? The Palace was home to the International Hockey League's Detroit Vipers from 1994 to 2001. In 1997, the team won the Turner Cup symbolizing the IHL championship. But the team couldn't attract a steady fan base.

Besides, Bill Davidson already owns the Tampa Bay Lightning. That is a money loser. Why does he need another?

# Who scored the biggest goal in Red Wings history?

TERRY The water bottle moved! The water bottle moved!

That is what rolled through my mind after Steve Yzerman blasted a 60-foot shot over the right shoulder of St. Louis Blues goaltender Jon Casey in Game 7 of the 1996 Western Conference semifinals. Yzerman glided just over the red line and launched a missile that hit the top corner of the net and made Casey's water bottle lying on top of the net jump as if it were alive.

I was pacing from the press area to a spot just behind the net and saw the dramatic goal from up close. It broke a 0-0 tie and sent the Wings to the Western Conference Finals where they lost to Colorado.

There was so much tension in that building. Fans wanted this game almost as much as they wanted to see the Lions in the Super Bowl. The two teams battled for much of the game in a tight checking contest. You knew early on this was going to be decided by a play or two.

The Wings were at the beginning of several championship runs, but there was the feeling they were going to choke another playoff series away. This was the same team that lost a playoff Game 7 to San Jose when goalie Chris Osgood mishandled a puck.

This town could not handle another setback.

That is why the celebration following the Yzerman goal was the loudest in Joe Louis Arena history. Players piled into the corner, and horns blew for several minutes while everybody savored this moment.

Wings fans love Yzerman, which made this goal even more special. They celebrate his every accomplishment, and this game was one of the

Was Steve Yzerman's Game 7 shot in 1996 clutch enough to be the top Red Wings' goal?

building blocks that helped make Yzerman one of the best leaders in hockey.

D R E W | The biggest goal came courtesy of the oldest guy on the ice. Had Igor Larionov, "The Old Professor," not ended Game 3 of the 2002 Stanley Cup Finals nearly 15 minutes into the third overtime, who knows how that series might have concluded? Who knows if the game would still be going on to this point four years later?

The predominant assumption remains that the Wings still would have claimed their third Stanley Cup in six seasons even if they had lost Game 3. Yeah, they were the better team. They had a collection of nine certain Hall of Famers who considered the Stanley Cup their destiny. The Wings had stars, whereas the Carolina Hurricanes were more starry-eyed, stunning everyone with their inaugural appearance in the championship round.

But you know as well as I do, Terry, how funky playoff hockey becomes with a little luck and a suddenly impenetrable goalie. The unthinkable has a way of becoming reality.

> "Who knows if [Game 3 of the 2002 finals] would still be going on to this point four years later?"

The Wings and Hurricanes were tied at one win apiece when the NHL's championship stage went south of the Mason-Dixon Line for the first time on June 8, 2002.

And the darn game just didn't want to end.

What began as Saturday evening ventured well into Sunday morning when the 41-year-old Larionov took a pass from linemate Tomas Holmstrom and made a quick move as he skated across the slot, causing Hurricanes forward Bates Battaglia to stumble just enough to give Larionov a little space to wreak havoc.

Larionov slipped a backhander past Carolina goalie Arturs Irbe, and the game finally ended.

That loss sucked the wind out of the Hurricanes. The Wings won the next two games and the Cup, but anybody who believes they easily disposed of Carolina is sadly mistaken. The Hurricanes believed the Wings' advanced age might have caught up with them in a best-of-seven series had they pushed them even longer on that long, long night in North Carolina and found a way to win.

Larionov became the oldest player in NHL history to score a goal in a Stanley Cup final when he scored the Wings' first goal in Game 3. And it might have seemed like another 41 years when he scored his second.

It is generally agreed that Terry Sawchuk, Steve Yzerman, Gordie Howe, and Nicklas Lidstrom belong on the Wings' all-time starting six. But who should be the left wing and second defenseman?

DREW   If you don't put Ted Lindsay on the team at left wing, do you want to be the one to tell him that he's not on it? Ol' Scarface is an old man today, but I still don't think you'd want to cross him or risk a right cross to the chops.

I'm not surprised you went with Fedorov, Terry. You consider yourself a little pretty boy like Sergei anyway. What's the common attraction? Is there a history of dating blond 16-year-old tennis players in your past?

Fedorov was hype. Lindsay was hockey.

Fedorov was flowing locks. Lindsay was broken teeth.

He never once backed down from a confrontation—even if it was a playful dig at opposing fans. The Wings went to Toronto for Game 4 of the first round of the 1952 Stanley Cup playoffs looking for a 4-0 sweep. Lindsay received death threats from Maple Leaf fans, promising he wouldn't get out of Maple Leaf Gardens that night alive if he played and the Wings won.

He played. The Wings swept the series and afterward, Lindsay skated out to center ice, wielded his stick as a machine gun, and pretended to open fire on the booing patrons.

Lindsay is sixth on the Wings' all-time scoring list with 728 points.

Now I must concede that are more similarities in personalities between our second defenseman, but how can you not go with a guy named "Black Jack" Stewart?

Jack Stewart was one of the initial pieces to the foundation that spawned the Wings' NFL dominance throughout the 1950s. He fittingly earned the name "Black Jack" because he was the darkness lurking at the blue line, preying on unsuspecting forwards entering the Wings' zone. He didn't hit. He crushed people. He once told reporters he got the name because after he delivered a rough check to an opponent, the guy got up off the ice and asked who just hit him with a blackjack.

Just ask Montreal's Elmer Lach.

Lach was still recovering from a broken jaw in the 1949 Stanley Cup first-round playoffs when Stewart delivered a heat-seeking elbow to his face, knocking him out of the remainder of the series. A Montreal sports columnist was so enraged that he assailed Stewart in what the writer considered a deliberate and malicious attack.

The Wings sued the paper for libel.

The case was eventually thrown out.

But Stewart's legend was born.

TERRY | I want to add size and speed to this team, so it can win in any era. That is why I would add Sergei Fedorov at left wing and my defenseman would be Vladimir Konstantinov.

Although Sergei Federov was dogged by Red Wings fans for being lazy while playing in the neutral zone, Federov controlled the game with masterful skating and passing that escaped many fans. The Soviet style of hockey concentrated more on puck possession. There was fluidity to Fedorov's game that made it look like he wasn't trying, but he was one of the game's better defensive forwards.

Federov was named the league's first European-born Most Valuable Player in 1994, the year that a herniated disk injury to Yzerman forced

Federov to assume more offensive responsibilities. And that only raised expectations further.

Fans kept waiting for him to pepper the league with 50-goal seasons. But he played a two-way game and did not need to score to dominate. Still, his 400 goals as a Red Wing are hard to ignore.

I will admit he could have and should have done more. But he helped the Wings to three Stanley Cups and played some of his better hockey during the playoffs.

In an era when the Wings were criticized for being too soft, Vladimir Konstantinov was a human land mine. Konstantinov could hit, and he played with a mean edge, making things uneasy for shooters. He resembled a safety in football: His opponents always had to look over their shoulder when coming across the middle.

I remember reading during the 1997 Stanley Cup Finals how big and tough the Philadelphia Flyers were. They were big, but they sure did not look tough, flinching every time Konstantinov hovered nearby.

But just days after the Wings' 1997 Stanley Cup victory, Konstantinov suffered a closed-head injury in a limousine accident. He clung to life for days but gradually improved. Konstantinov remains a paraplegic although he vows to walk and skate someday.

Konstantinov was the emotional inspiration for the Wings' successful Stanley Cup defense in 1998. "Believe" became the battle cry, and after the team finished a four-game sweep of Washington in the nation's capital, they wheeled out Konstantinov so he could celebrate with his teammates.

If you never saw him play, you might feel sorry for him. But when he hit the ice, the dude made the best and toughest players in the league look over their shoulder. He was always lurking, ready to land the heavy hit.

Who was the Red Wings' biggest Original Six rival?

DREW | *Sacre bleu!* It's Les Canadiens!

When the Wings and Montreal played in their often-classic playoff series through the 1950s, it was as much a cultural war as it was a battle for hockey supremacy. The French-speaking populace in Quebec was considered second-rate citizens from Canada's majority English-speaking ruling class. The Canadiens' rise to hockey's elite as well as their incorporating French-Canadian stars such as Maurice "Rocket" Richard endeared them to the peasant class. The Wings were the Canadiens' biggest Stanley Cup challenger in the 1950s and in the minds of the French-Canadians, the Wings and the popularity of stars Gordie Howe, Ted Lindsay, Sid Abel, and Terry Sawchuk represented the dominance of English-speaking rule.

They faced each other six times in the Stanley Cup playoffs during that decade—four times in the finals. The series record was three wins apiece for each franchise, but each Detroit series win came in the finals, resulting in a Stanley Cup and further fueling the rivalry.

But the two teams were indelibly conjoined in one of the ugliest incidents in NHL history on March 17, 1955.

The city of Montreal was still ticked off that NHL commissioner Clarence Campbell suspended the Rocket for the duration of the regular season and the playoffs two weeks earlier after Richard took a hockey stick to the head of Boston's Hal Laycoe. The Montreal fans believed the severity of Campbell's punishment was attributed more to cultural prejudice. Campbell attended the first playoff game between the Wings and Canadiens at the Montreal Forum and was immediately besieged with eggs, programs, shoes, and anything else that was available to Canadiens fans. When a smoke bomb went off inside the arena, officials cancelled the game, giving the Wings a victory via forfeit.

The crowd's rancor took to the streets of Montreal, causing a riot responsible for more than $500,000 in property damage.

T E R R Y | One of my high school buddies often wore a Montreal Canadiens sweater to school and like you, Boodini, he tried to convince me they were the Wings' biggest rival.

I simply told him that the fact he was allowed to wear a Canadiens sweater in Detroit without getting beat up provided enough evidence that the Toronto Maple Leafs, not the Canadiens, were the Wings' biggest rival.

We'd take your lunch money away and bound and gag you in the middle of Grand River if you wore a Maple Leafs sweater.

Wings–Maple Leafs games were events. They used to battle eight times a year and usually games ended in blood baths. And that was in the stands.

Maple Leafs fans crowded the tunnel from Canada for games at Olympia because there were fans in western Ontario who were split in their allegiance between the Red Wings and Leafs. It was not unusual to hear busloads of people cheering or jeering both the Wings and Leafs.

That added to the intrigue. When you walked in downtown Windsor or London, you never knew if you were rubbing elbows with Leafs or Wings fans.

The Canadiens were far and away the best franchise during the Original Six era. The Leafs and Wings were often fighting over table scraps.

Old timers can't forget how Maple Leafs goalie Turk Broda shut down the Wings' "Production Line" of Gordie Howe, Sid Abel, and Ted Lindsey, leading the Leafs to their third straight Stanley Cup in 1949.

And who can forget the 1993 playoffs when Toronto battled from a 3-1 deficit to beat the Wings in the playoffs, winning Game 7 at Joe Louis Arena? I still hate those sons of bit– Oops! See how worked up I got? I almost turned this family publication R-rated.

But you get the picture. The Leafs were the Wings' nemesis.

Sadly, the NHL pushed the Wings to the Western Conference while the Canadiens and Maple Leafs remain in the East. Now these teams sometimes only play once a year. That is a tragedy and takes something away from the league.

 # Who would have won in a best-of-seven Series between the 1968 and 1984 Tigers?

TERRY The 1984 Tigers were the better team. But the 1968 Tigers (103-59) had the biggest hearts in baseball. If games were seven innings long, the 1968 team would have finished well out of the pennant hunt. But these dogs never died. They rallied 35 times to win games when trailing in the seventh inning. They trailed St. Louis 3-1 in the World Series but won the final three games to take the crown.

And you want to talk tough? In 1967 they lost the pennant on the final day of the season in the aftermath of a riot where they were forced to travel through smoldering neighborhoods to get to the ballpark. The following season they finished 12 games ahead of the pack to win the final true pennant. In 1969 Major League Baseball changed to the division system.

People say this was a light-hitting team. It is true the Tigers batted .235, but the league average was just .230. Yet the Tigers had hitters to fear. Willie Horton (36 home runs), Stormin' Norman Cash (25 home runs), and Bill Freehan (25 home runs) displayed good power. Jim Northrup led the team with 90 RBI, and he was noted for the number of grand slam home runs he hit. Of course, I would also have Al Kaline in right field for this hypothetical series. But remember Kaline missed five weeks of the 1968 season with a fractured forearm after being hit by a pitch, and despite that loss, the Tigers were strong at the plate.

The 1968 team would win with pitching. Denny McLain (31–6) was the first man to win 30 games in 30 years. He was backed by Mickey Lolich (17–9) and Earl Wilson (13–12), who was coming off a 22-win season.

I was there the night the Tigers clinched the pennant 2–1 against the New York Yankees. In typical fashion they did not score much, and Joe Sparma was wild, but they rallied to find a way to win at the end.

The 1968 Tigers in seven, of course. They always made things difficult.

D R E W | The "Bless You Boys" of 1984 would have beaten the 1968 team, because of its more balanced offensive lineup. The top five hitters were an opposing manager's nightmare, because you couldn't manipulate your pitching staff to take advantage of any perceived weaknesses on any side of the plate.

That was how left-hander Mickey Lolich dominated St. Louis in the 1968 World Series, because the bulk of the Cardinals' offensive pop was left-handed. Lolich would have experienced far more difficulty navigating around the right-handed punch of Alan Trammell in the No. 2 spot, catcher Lance Parrish at the cleanup hole, and center fielder Chet Lemon at No. 6.

It wouldn't have been any easier for right-hander Denny McLain, because 1984 Tigers manager Sparky Anderson had lefty bats at leadoff, No. 3, and No. 5 in the lineup. And Lou Whitaker, Kirk Gibson, and Darrell Evans had a combined 56 home runs and 210 RBI during that championship season.

That offensive balance would have eventually caught up to McLain and Lolich.

The only big power bat in the 1968 lineup was Willie Horton, who led the team with 36 homers that season. Horton was also a free swinger, making him more vulnerable to Jack Morris's split-fingered fastball which, when thrown properly, fell off the table just before crossing the plate, fooling batters into swinging meekly.

The game was also more specialized in 1984 than it was in 1968. McLain and Lolich were more likely to finish what they started then as opposed to Aurelio Lopez, an eighth-inning setup man, and Willie Hernandez, the Tigers' closer, who had specific responsibilities.

The Tigers acquired Hernandez and defensive specialist, first baseman Dave Bergmann, from the Philadelphia Phillies just weeks before the start of the 1984 season. Hernandez was never before entrusted with the closer's role. But he saved 32 games in 33 save opportunities, winning both the American League Cy Young and Most Valuable Player awards.

The 1984 bullpen would have held any lead the team built for them.

The 1984 Tigers win in six games.

# Who would join Ty Cobb in center **and Al Kaline in right** as the left fielder on the **all-time Detroit team?**

DREW | How can you not have an all-time outfield full of Hall of Famers? Henry (Heinie) Manush played for six teams in 17 years, but his first five seasons were with the Tigers. Manush's timing wasn't the best. The "dead ball" era of baseball was taking its final breaths, and here was a *slap hitter,* somebody who could punch the ball to any part of the field at his choosing, coming into the game at the start of the free-swinging home run era.

The Tigers' outfield was pretty crowded during Manush's rookie season in 1923. Cobb was approaching the twilight of his great career. He was so revered that the organization made him player/manager. And there was another future Hall of Famer in right field, Harry Heilman.

It could have been a very intimidating circumstance for a young player. Manush struggled in his first three seasons, splitting time with Bobby Veach in left field. But Manush not only won the starting left fielder's job in his fourth season, he won the American League batting title with a .378 average. He trailed Babe Ruth and teammate Heilman heading into the season's final day, but Manush went six-for-nine in a doubleheader. It was the first of five times during his career that Manush finished among the top five in league batting.

Cobb thought that Manush was the mirror image of himself—gritty and hard-nosed. And he never lost faith in Manush despite his early struggles, and Manush was devotedly loyal to Cobb. That created a conflict when the Tigers replaced Cobb at manager with George Moriarty prior to the 1927 season. Manush played well that first season under Moriarty, but constant run-ins with his manager forced the Tigers to make a choice.

And, of course, they made the wrong one.

They traded Manush to the St. Louis Browns for what amounted to a bucket of baseballs.

Manush remained one of the game's more reliable hitters, gaining entry into the Hall of Fame in 1964 through the veteran's committee.

TERRY | I once sat in the stands keeping score on my Tigers scorecard. Willie Horton came up to the plate, and I put HR besides his name for home run. That is how certain I was about Horton at the plate.

Horton was a powerful slugger (325 home runs and 1,163 runs batted in) and stepped up during the big moments. He batted .304 during the 1968 World Series and hit a home run in Game 2. But his biggest moment came in the field. Horton was always criticized for his defense. But I thought it was better than writers gave him credit for.

They never seemed to forgive him for coming into spring training a few pounds over his playing weight.

In Game 5 of the Series, he nailed speedy St. Louis Cardinals outfielder Lou Brock with a picture-perfect throw to catcher Bill Freehan, who stood his ground and tagged Brock out. The Cards led the series 3-1 at the time, but the play sparked the Tigers, and they rallied from a 3-2 deficit to win the game 5-3 and the Series in seven games.

Everybody talked about the pitching matchups of Bob Gibson and Denny McLain. They also praise Mickey Lolich for winning three games. But Horton's defense turned the tide, and that photo of Brock colliding with Freehan is one of the most famous photos in Detroit history.

Everybody talked about how surprised they were that Horton made the throw. It did not surprise me at all.

He lasted eight more seasons with the Tigers before being traded to Texas for pitcher Steve Foucault. Horton bounced around until 1979 when he won Comeback Player of the Year by hitting 29 home runs and driving in 109 runs with Seattle.

Horton grew up in Detroit and loved this city. That's why he moved back and is a consultant with the Tigers in addition to business interests he has here. He tried to calm crowds down during the 1968 riots while wearing his Tigers uniform. Horton also opened up a bar called Club 23.

There was a lot of debate whether Horton should have a statue placed in center field at Comerica. It is an easy choice. He not only qualifies as the Tigers' best left fielder, but he made a difference in the community.

By the way, Horton blasted one to left field that day I penciled him in for a home run, missing it by 10 feet with a foul blast.

So he wasn't perfect.

# Who was the all-time Tigers catcher?

TERRY Defense wins games. That is why Tigers catcher Bill Freehan was the best in club history.

He was an 11-time All-Star and shares Major League Baseball's all-time highest fielder percentage by a catcher (.993) along with Elston Howard. He also worked on his game. Freehan signed a $100,000 bonus but led the American Association in pass balls in 1962.

But he worked with Hall of Fame catcher Rick Ferrell, who showed him tips on becoming the best defensive catcher in baseball.

We talk about the wonderful throw Willie Horton made to the plate in Game 5 to nail St. Louis Cardinals speed man Lou Brock. But Freehan was the guy who caught the ball and hung on while Brock plowed into him.

Freehan was part of one of the biggest plays in Tigers history, because he was big and strong and did not back down.

But his biggest asset was the way he handled pitchers. He knew how to settle down wild men like Denny McLain, rev up the calm Mickey Lolich, and get the best out of the sensitive Joe Sparma.

It takes skill to get the best out of three diverse personalities. Now we see why he went on to become the baseball coach at the University of Michigan. He got his training with the Tigers.

Freehan was never a great hitter, but he did bop 200 home runs and knocked in 758 runs. Freehan wrote a controversial book called *Behind the Mask* in which he revealed some clubhouse secrets that involved Mayo Smith and Denny McLain.

The book may have led to Smith's getting fired and McLain's being traded to the Washington Senators. For the most part he was a team player, willing to play despite constant leg and back pain. In 1968 he set an American League record by getting hit by 24 pitches.

Now that's taking one for the team.

DREW | Mickey Mantle was named after Mickey Cochrane. That alone might be worthy of deity status.

Cochrane was already one of the game's premier catchers with the Philadelphia Athletics, but the A's were in need of money, so the Tigers came to their rescue. The Tigers traded catcher Johnny Pasek, but more importantly, cut a check for $100,000 to the A's for Cochrane, a future Hall of Famer. Don't diminish his standing as the franchise's top catcher simply because he wasn't an original product of the system and gradually worked his way up to the parent club. Most baseball experts generally regard "Black Mike" as the game's best catcher of the 1920s and 1930s.

> "[Mickey Cochrane] was a guy who still excelled at the toughest position on the field while managing the Tigers to two American League pennants."

But here's where you lose your argument, Terry, the Tigers made Cochrane a player/manager soon after they acquired him. So here was a guy who still excelled at the toughest position on the field while managing the Tigers to two American League pennants in his first two years.

They lost to the St. Louis Cardinals in the seventh game of the 1934 fall classic, but they defeated the Chicago Cubs in 1935 to give the Tigers their first World Series championship.

And the only reason he only played four years in Detroit was that Cochrane almost died on May 25, 1937, at Yankee Stadium when a fastball from New York Yankees pitcher Bump Hadley hit him in the head, just barely missing his temple. The impact was so forceful that it left a visible dent in his skull. Priests administered last rites when Cochrane was slow to regain consciousness after a couple of days in a New York hospital's intensive care.

He eventually recovered, but sadly, Cochrane became gun-shy in the batter's box after that harrowing scare. He retired as a player following the 1937 season, but remained as the Tigers' manager through 1938.

Who had the best season ever for a Tigers closer?

DREW Nobody had a better season than John Hiller in 1973 with a then-major league record of 38 saves, because nobody ever had to endure as much as the crafty left-hander did to get to the mound that season.

Hiller shouldn't have pitched that season. He probably shouldn't have been alive.

Hiller was on a hunting trip near his Duluth, Minnesota, home in January 1971, when he experienced a burning sensation in his chest. He thought it was a bad case of heartburn, and it couldn't have been "the other thing," because he was too young to have a heart attack. He was three months shy of his 28th birthday. But offseason conditioning wasn't a big thing for pitchers during that era. Hiller was overweight and a heavy smoker, and wasn't shy about slamming down a few brews.

He suffered a massive heart attack.

Hiller underwent surgery, having seven feet of his intestine removed in an effort to alleviate high cholesterol problems that his doctors believed contributed to his heart problems.

Hiller approached the Tigers about pitching in 1972, but the organization was understandably hesitant. No Major League Baseball player had ever suffered a heart attack and later returned to the active roster. But further intensifying the Tigers' fears was the sudden death of Detroit Lions receiver Chuck Hughes from a heart attack during an NFL game on October 24, 1971.

Hiller didn't give up. He convinced the Tigers to let him pitch batting practice during the 1972 season. And then on July 8, 1972, 18 months after nearly dying from a heart attack, Hiller pitched one inning in a 5-2 Tigers loss to the Chicago White Sox.

There was no stopping Hiller. He became the Tigers' primary closer in 1973.

And although his record saves total has been eclipsed many times over the last 30 years, Hiller didn't get the benefit of the "cheap" saves of his successors. It's ridiculous that a closer gets credit for a save for entering the game in the ninth inning with a three-run lead. The Hall of Fame developed what it called "a tough save" criteria to measure the achievements of those players from different eras. A tough save constitutes entering the game with at least the tying run on base. Every save situation Hiller had in 1973 was classified as a tough save.

Does your boy meet that standard, Foster?

T E R R Y | Willie Hernandez always wanted to be a closer. Thankfully for the Tigers, the Chicago Cubs and Philadelphia Phillies did not give him the chance. You would think he had earned that role after three scoreless setup outings in the 1983 World Series for Philadelphia.

But the Phillies insisted on keeping him in the setup role. Hernandez complained, and the Tigers gave up Glen Wilson and John Wockenfuss for Dave Bergman and Hernandez.

He took off running, confusing American League hitters in 1984 with an assortment of screwballs, sinking fastballs, and curves. People did not think he threw hard, but he did. It's just that hitters did not know what was coming and they were off balance. How many times did we see batters take weak swings at outside pitches or get turned inside out by inside screwballs?

He converted a record 32 consecutive save opportunities. He finished the season 9-3 with a 1.92 earned run average and won the

Cy Young and Most Valuable Player awards. He was instrumental in the Tigers' 35-5 start.

John Hiller overcame a lot, but Hernandez was the best pitcher in baseball that year. How can that not be the all-time top performance?

In the American League Championship Series he appeared in all three games and earned a save in the clincher against Kansas City. And in the World Series he pitched in three of five games against San Diego and earned two saves.

He followed up the championship season with 30 and 24 saves the following seasons, but was on the decline. He was eventually replaced by Mike Henneman.

That's not bad for a former first baseman. Hernandez became a pitcher only because the Puerto Rican team he played for needed pitching. In his first outing he pitched a seven-hit shutout, and the Tigers closer of the future was born, even after a few bumps along the way.

# Who is your all-time
Tigers second baseman–
Charlie Gehringer
or Lou Whitaker?

DREW During Major League Baseball's centennial celebration in 1969, a panel of veteran baseball writers voted Gehringer the greatest living second baseman in baseball history. It's believed that former pitching great Lefty Gomez gave Gehringer the moniker "The Mechanical Man" because of reliable consistency. Former teammate and fellow Hall of Famer Hank Greenberg said in his biography *Hank Greenberg* that the nickname fit Gehringer perfectly because "you'd wind him up Opening Day and then forget about it the rest of the season."

Whitaker and Gehringer were mirror images of each other defensively—fluidly agile and sure handed. And, granted, the offensive demands of second basemen changed during Whitaker's time when ballparks gradually shrunk and power numbers increased.

But how many American League Most Valuable Player awards did Whitaker win?

The answer is zip.

Gehringer won the AL MVP in 1937 when he led the league with a .371 batting average.

Gehringer is third among the Tigers' all-time hit leaders with 2,839—nearly 500 hits more than Whitaker. He's ranked fourth all-time in runs batted in (1,427), the highest-ranked infielder in that category. He's ranked third in total runs scored (1,774), nearly 400 more than Whitaker.

Gehringer was an underappreciated power source. Six times during his career, he hit 15 or more home runs in a season. That was considered pretty good power production for a middle infielder in the first half of the 20th century.

Lou was sweet and silky smooth, but Gehringer might have been the second-most complete ballplayer to ever wear the Old English D—after Ty Cobb, of course. Did Whitaker ever have a season comparable to Gehringer's 1929 season when "The Mechanical Man" led the AL in eight categories, including hits, runs, doubles, triples, and stolen bases?

But awarding two separate MVP awards for the two leagues wasn't mandatory from 1922 to 1929. The Chicago Cubs' Rogers Hornsby was considered the game's best player that season—period—and there was no American League recognition that season.

That policy ended after that season. But it was a year too late to help Gehringer.

TERRY "Sweet Lou" Whitaker played two seasons in the minors at third base. But the conversion to second base was both fruitful and sweet for the smooth fielder when he joined the Tigers. He made everything look easy and was unjustly criticized for taking it easy. He can't help it that he was smooth as silk playing next to a bunch of clunkers.

His practice habits were not the best in spring training, but he lost weight during the season and held up better than most.

Whitaker and Joe Morgan are the only two men to play 2,000 games at second base, get 2,000 hits, and hit 200 home runs. He won three Gold Gloves and made five All-Star teams.

Whitaker also was one of the most clutch hitters of all time. During the Tigers' 35-5 run in 1984, Whitaker spliced in a 10-game hitting streak during which he hit .442.

He led all players by scoring six runs in the World Series against San Diego, led both teams with 18 assists, and did not make an error in 33 chances.

Drew, you ask the question did Whitaker ever have a season like Charlie Gehringer's 1929 season in which he led the American League in eight offensive categories?

That answer is no. But put Whitaker in the same situation in the same season and he would have done the same thing. Oh wait. That is impossible because Gehringer played in an era that did not allow black ballplayers.

I'm sorry. A bunch of those old records are tainted because Major League Baseball did not include everybody who could play the game.

Whitaker was a devout Jehovah's Witness and was a little standoffish to the media. He sometimes did not talk, and certain media members held that against him. He is a borderline Hall of Fame second baseman, who could field with the best of them.

We should not hold it against him for being a little weird. Lou was sweet when he fielded the ball. And he was also the Tigers' best second baseman.

Do Alan Trammell
and Lou Whitaker
belong in Baseball's
Hall of Fame?

DREW | No, they don't.

It's easy to fall for the sappiness of sentimentality. They were the young twins who came up together, forming the foundation for a rebirth that culminated in the 1984 World Series championship and a divisional title in 1987—the last championship in the franchise's history.

But the Hall of Fame must be reserved for those who were unquestioned standouts at their respective positions during their era, and Trammell's and Whitaker's careers don't meet that standard. Neither amassed 2,500 career hits, nor did they particularly redefine their position, transcending the game. Perhaps if Whitaker could have gotten 300 home runs, unheard of for a second baseman's career (at least until the start of the so-called Steriods Era in 1995), he could have made an argument.

Just playing more games together than any other "keystone combination," in major league history is not worthy of Hall of Fame distinction.

Whitaker hit more home runs than Joe Morgan, the last second baseman voted into the Hall of Fame in 1990. And that's always brought up as validation of Whitaker's credentials, but Morgan was an MVP award winner in 1972. He was an integral piece of the Big Red

Machine, which won three National League pennants and two World Series in five years.

Baltimore's Cal Ripken Jr. and St. Louis's Ozzie Smith were the dominating shortstops of the 1980s, overwhelming Trammell in the public's baseball conscience. Ripken brought an offensive force to the position that paved the way for successors such as Alex Rodriguez, Derek Jeter, and Nomar Garciaparra.

Don't whine about how Trammell and Whitaker were supposedly victims of low media coverage. Just accept the fact that their greatness was restricted to a sole franchise and that all alone is worth celebrating.

TERRY | Let me get this straight. The Baseball Hall of Fame inducts its best individual players. And it includes its biggest moments, biggest home runs, and even a couple of songs, but it does not include its best double-play combination of all time?

That makes no sense.

The Hall of Fame is about including the best of the best. Trammell and Whitaker played lockdown defense at shortstop and second base for nearly two decades. Geez, it is hard to find couples married for that long.

Here is what's wrong with the baseball elite. If you hit the ball, you get in the Hall of Fame. If you prevent people from scoring, it does not matter. Baseball is the only sport where defense rarely counts toward deciding the best players. And that is wrong. Trammell's fielding percentage of .977 is higher than any shortstop in the Hall of Fame.

Whitaker and Joe Morgan are the only second basemen with 2,000 hits, 2,000 games, and 200 home runs. And need I remind you one more time that Whitaker and Trammell were the best double-play combination in baseball history?

Yet there is no room for them in the Hall of Fame?

That is baffling. So you mean to tell me that if they were both career .300 hitters, but let balls bounce off their legs they'd have a better shot at the Hall of Fame?

Well, that is the message baseball is sending.

Trammell and Whitaker made ballet together in the field for 1,918 games, an American League record. Both were instrumental in the Tigers' 1984 World Series victory. Trammell was Most Valuable Player after smacking two home runs and batting .450. Whitaker was perfect in the field and scored six runs.

If you want to exclude them as individuals, that is fine. But together they were the best. Cooperstown needs to reserve a spot for them.

In a Game 7, which Tiger do you want on the mound— Mickey Lolich or Jack Morris?

TERRY | Give me the donut man. Both were workhorses who logged monster innings during their career. I'd take either.

But what is the toughest thing to find in baseball? It is a flame-throwing left-handed pitcher. Teams would give their right arm (pardon the pun) for that. Lolich outgunned the great Bob Gibson in the 1968 World Series in Game 7 4-1 on two days' rest.

The rolly-polly Lolich shined brighter than Gibson and Denny McLain who won 31 games that season. He was a pressure pitcher who did not mind playing second fiddle.

Tigers manager Mayo Smith asked Lolich to pitch five innings in Game 7 after he'd already pitched complete games in Games 2 and 5. After the fifth inning Lolich thought he was finished. But Smith said, "Can you give me another?"

He asked Lolich the same question after each inning, and Lolich nodded his head yes each inning.

Here is what Smith did not know. Lolich pitched with an infected groin. He told his catcher, Bill Freehan, but kept the information from Smith because he wanted to gut it out.

Lolich might not have been the pitcher he was if not for a falling motorcycle. He was born right-handed, but when he was a toddler, he ran his tricycle into a motorcycle, toppling it over, and broke his left collarbone. Doctors recommended that Lolich throw left-handed to straighten it out. That might explain his big, side-winding delivery.

You want to give the ball to Lolich in any situation because he is not afraid to pitch a lot of innings. He laughs at today's pitchers who are praised for pitching 200 innings in a season, because he did it 12 times in his career. And did I mention he cracked 300 innings four times?

Lolich won 20 games twice and finished with 217 career victories.

People made fun of his weight, but I'm convinced that is what made Lolich tick. He was a hero to the common man and he did not need much rest to pitch a commanding game.

Lolich is my guy to pitch the seventh game. Heck, he could probably do it today.

D R E W | Why am I not surprised that somebody with an obvious affinity for donuts would take Lolich in this argument?

Put the ball in Morris's hand.

Morris wasn't a gentleman. Bluntly put—he was a jerk far too often. But I'm not looking for a charm school valedictorian in that situation. I want somebody who despises losing as much as he cherishes winning. And that's why Morris was the game's premier "money" pitcher during his era.

Lolich was brilliant in the Tigers' 1968 World Series triumph over the St. Louis Cardinals.

But as dominating as Morris was when he won both of his starts in the Tigers' 1984 romp over the San Diego Padres, he was even more overpowering when he led the Minnesota Twins to the world championship against the Atlanta Braves in 1991—seven years later.

Morris got stronger with time. He gained more on his fastball as he got into later innings. That's what you need in a must-win Game 7, Terry.

Consider these totals from Morris's first two World Series performances. He was 4-0 with three complete games, a 1.23 earned run average and he averaged 8⅓ innings in his five starts. He had an ERA of 2.00 with the Tigers in 1984 and an ERA of 1.17 with the Twins in 1991.

And although everyone in Detroit holds Lolich's Game 7 in Busch Stadium in 1968 very near and dear to his or her heart, Morris remains indelibly etched in the baseball conscience for that October evening in 1991 when he took the ball against the Braves in Game 7 and didn't give it up for 10 innings.

The Twins won the Series with a 1-0 win when they scored in the bottom of the 10th, but everyone should understand that the Twins still had nobody ready in the bullpen. If the scoreless tie went to the top of the 11th inning, Morris would have taken the ball and still wouldn't have lost much off of his fastball.

Was Jack Morris enough of a gamer to grit his way through a game when everything was on the line?

 # Who deserves the next statue at at Comerica Park?

DREW | Now here is where Alan Trammell and Lou Whitaker receive their justified recognition. Retire their numbers—Nos. 1 and 3—and erect a monument to their reliability for almost 20 years. A marble replication of Trammell and Whitaker turning the double play would be a fitting tribute to what both meant to this team and this city.

They're not Hall of Famers, but they're certainly part of the Detroit sports' royal lineage. During Tiger Stadium's closing ceremonies in 1999, the living history of one of baseball's oldest franchises filled the grounds on which Ty Cobb, Babe Ruth, and Ted Williams once walked.

But the loudest roar was reserved for the last introduction—when Trammell and Whitaker came out together. Inseparable in Tigers fans' heart until the end, it didn't make sense when Trammell remained in the game for a year later in 1996 after Whitaker retired in 1995. It just wasn't right.

Individually, they were fine ballplayers whose fundamentals were so sound that their talents were easily taken for granted, especially from the national baseball media elite. But they should be honored collectively, because that's how they're remembered.

TERRY | One of the most joyous scenes in Detroit history came after Game 7 of the 1968 World Series when Mickey Lolich jumped into the arms of catcher Bill Freehan after Freehan caught a foul pop up from the St. Louis Cardinals' Tim McCarver for the final out.

That moment should be frozen in time with a bronzed statue in Center Field at Comerica Park. That scene represented so much during a troubled time in our history. The city was divided between black and white. Part of Detroit lay in ruins after the riot.

But this victory represented the underdog coming back from the brink of elimination. Our city is always behind and always trying to catch up, but it never dies. It lives another day because so many people refuse to give up no matter how badly things look.

The Tigers trailed the powerful St. Louis Cardinals three games to one and were behind in Game 5 before Willie Horton threw Lou Brock out at the plate. Before that play the city anticipated a World Series loss.

When Lolich jumped into Freehan's arms, it showed the fighting spirit of Detroit. We all remember where we were at that moment. I was at Ford Hospital after breaking out in a terrible rash that required hospitalization and lots of smelly lotion.

I itched for several days, but I didn't feel it the day the Tigers polished off the Cardinals. All of our fears, worries, and heartaches disappeared that day. The Tigers were World Series champions, and that meant the world to us. We were healing and trying to fight for another day.

That was what the Tigers had done all season. They fell behind and kept fighting until the rest of Major League Baseball gave up. That was our moment, our time to shine.

And it needs to be a reminder of what Detroit can become with hard work. We should never give up until we can jump and embrace one another in triumph.

# What was the most memorable/dramatic Tigers' home run ever?

TERRY | The grand slam home run utility man Rob Fick hit in September 1999 did not win a ball game. It did not break any tension.

But that home run said goodbye to an old friend. It was the final home run in Tiger Stadium. It did not matter that the Tigers beat Kansas City 8-2.

It was the exclamation point for the tired old lady on the corner of Michigan and Trumbull. People clapped. They cried and they tried to hang onto the memories of 6,873 regular-season games, 35 postseason games, and three All-Star Games.

This was a stadium that meant so much that fans formed The Tiger Stadium Fan Club and hugged the stadium to try to save it. Whenever folks talk about the final day, they talk about that home run.

It was a fitting present to a building that gave people so much joy.

Dramatic? Perhaps not. But the home run was filled with drama. As I watched the game from the third-level press box, I sensed something magic was going to happen.

It came from a player with little legacy. But it did not matter who hit it. This building deserved a nice farewell.

Babe Ruth hit his 700th home run here. Lou Gehrig took himself out of the lineup after playing in 2,130 consecutive games, and Denny McLain won his 30th game here in 1968.

Fick batted just 41 times that season as a late-season callup and hit just three home runs. He played five seasons with the Tigers and hit just 45 home runs before being traded to Atlanta.

After his Tiger Stadium home run, former and current Tiger players tossed autographed balls into the stands. Home plate was removed and taken to Comerica Park. And people cheered for the final goodbye.

They will remember the final pitch, the final celebration, and more importantly, the final home run by Flick.

D R E W | Back in the day when the only performance enhancer was a couple double cheeseburgers, the 50-homer plateau actually stood for something. It was considered a feat of Herculean status, and Cecil Fielder's flirtation with 50 homers in the 1990 season put the Tigers on the national baseball radar.

Fielder hit his 50th and 51st home runs on October, 3, 1990, in Tiger Stadium—the season's final day—becoming the 11th major leaguer to belt 50 home runs in a season and the first American Leaguer to attain that standard since 1961 when New York Yankees' Roger Maris and Mickey Mantle did it, captivating the nation with their chase of Babe Ruth's single-season home run record of 60.

There was a buzz at Tiger Stadium that night that hadn't been there since that September afternoon in 1968 when Denny McLain looked for his 30th win. There was fear that pitchers wouldn't give Fielder anything tantalizing to hit, perhaps even intentionally walking him to avoid surrendering the record-making dinger.

The city needed that season. It helped raise Detroit off the mat, giving it a little national acclaim for something not related to FBI crime reports.

The Tigers signed Fielder to a two-year contract the previous offseason. The big fella had struggled for three years in Toronto. His weight fluctuated to just south of 300 pounds. But Fielder signed with the Hanshin Tigers in 1989 and blasted 38 homers. Detroit took a chance, signing Fielder to a two-year contract.

It was one of the Tigers' better free agent moves when you consider that Fielder finished second in the American League Most

Valuable Player voting in the 1990, placing behind Oakland's Rickey Henderson, and 1991, finishing behind Baltimore's Cal Ripken Jr.

Fielder was only the second player to hit 50 dingers in a season in the previous 13 years. And according to statistics from TheBaseballPage.com, players surpassed 50 home runs in a season just 17 times from 1900 to 1994. But from 1994 to 2005, the 50-homer plateau was reached 18 times.

Got steroids, anyone?

Fielder was the only hitter to ever clear the left field roof at Tiger Stadium, and that special season brings back fond memories when the only juice in the game was a cold, frothy one after the game.

Will Alan Trammell's unsuccessful stint as Tigers manager ruin his long-term reputation as a player?

DREW How could I think his reputation is harmed any if I'm advocating a statue of Lou Whitaker and him beyond the center field wall at Comerica Park? It wouldn't be a statue of him walking out to the mound to change pitchers for the third time that inning.

There were concerns regarding this very question when he took over the frayed reins of this team in the fall of 2002. He was brought in because of his brand name. The strategy was returning the ghosts of 1984—Trammell, Kirk Gibson as the bench coach, and Lance Parrish as the bullpen coach. If you brought the past back, having them energetically ride into town like a modern-day cavalry, then it just might divert the fans' attention away from the wretched present situation.

Trammell was overmatched as the Tigers manager. It was on-the-job training. The hope was that he would learn with the team. But despite all the criticism Trammell endured as a manager, there was never any residual blemish upon his playing career as a Tiger.

You know the saying, What have you done for me lately?

TERRY | Many of us will remember Trammell for being one of the best shortstops in the game. But most don't remember what he did in 1984 when he was the World Series' Most Valuable Player. All they know is he failed as a manager, and the Tigers regressed under him.

That is one reason some did not want Trammell taking the Tigers job. We knew this team was not ready to win no matter who was in charge. And sadly I suspect that Trammell did not have full powers anyway. It seems as though president Dave Dombrowski, not Tram, called a lot of the shots.

Trammell lost control of the dressing room, because he could not control Pudge Rodriguez who used to curse the man in front of the team. Obviously, Rodriguez did not know what Trammell meant to the rest of us. He simply viewed him as a man he did not respect as a manager.

The players sure did not give him the proper respect. We heard few glowing testimonies of Trammell when his ship crashed.

Dombrowski sure didn't show respect. He let Trammell linger in the wind, although he knew he was not going to retain him.

And the sports fans certainly did not cut him much slack. All we heard on talk radio was what a failure he was. I respect Tram for what he was. Sadly, I am in the minority.

He is now remembered for failure rather than the two decades of success and happiness he gave this town.

What was the most dramatic All-Star Game home run in Detroit history?

DREW — Ted Williams stood poised at the cusp of legendary status when he came to Briggs Stadium for Major League Baseball's ninth All-Star Game on July 8, 1941. The Boston Red Sox slugger, dubbed "The Splendid Splinter" for his smooth batting stroke, was participating in his second midsummer classic. He batted cleanup in the order behind the Yankees' Joe DiMaggio.

The American League trailed the National League 5-3 in the bottom of the ninth with one out when two singles and a walk loaded the bases for DiMaggio. He hit the ball sharply to shortstop Eddie Miller for a possible game-ending double play. Miller flipped the ball to second baseman Billy Herman, but Herman's relay was just wide of first base. A runner scored, DiMaggio was safe at first, and up came Teddy Ballgame with two runners aboard.

In later years when recalling the moment, Williams said he was waiting for the fastball.

He didn't wait long.

Williams sent the first pitch deep into Briggs Stadium's upper right field seats, giving the American League a dramatic 7-5 win. The grainy black-and-white film images of the lanky Williams happily skipping along the base paths remain one of the All-Star Game's more stirring memories.

There was never a bigger All-Star homer in Detroit when you consider that it was a game-winner, but also when you factor in the state of America at that time. Historians look back upon 1941 as a seminal year in American sports. By year's end, the United States was into World War II after the attack on Pearl Harbor. A year later, baseball stars like Williams and DiMaggio would enlist in the armed services. But everyone could fondly recall the baseball memories of that special summer of 1941 when Williams became the last major leaguer to bat .400 in a season and DiMaggio hit safely in 56 consecutive games—a record that still stood through the 2005 season.

TERRY | Oakland A's slugger Reggie Jackson hit a home run that packed enough punch to be included on his Baseball Hall of Fame plaque in Cooperstown. And that's saying something, considering all he accomplished as one of baseball's all-time great sluggers.

He was nicknamed "Mr. October" for his World Series heroics, but became Mr. July during the 1971 All-Star Game. There were six home runs hit by six future Hall of Fame baseball players, but everybody talks about Jackson's one-out, third-inning shot off Pittsburgh Pirates pitcher Dock Ellis, which cleared the right-center field roof, hit a light transformer 94 feet in the air, and drew cheers that still last today.

"People always ask me about that one," Jackson told me during a visit to Detroit.

"Historians estimate the blast at 540 feet. The only thing missing were sparks shooting from the light tower."

Historians estimate the blast at 540 feet. The only thing missing were sparks shooting from the light tower. In the 77-year history of the stadium, only 19 players for a total of 28 times cleared the Tiger Stadium roof.

Jackson once said, "God, do I love to hit that little round sum-bitch out of the park and make 'em say, 'Wow!'"

Many stood in amazement at the late fireworks that came nine days after the Fourth of July.

The home run sparked a four-run inning that propelled the American League to a 6-4 victory over the National Leaguers before 53,559 fans, snapping an eight-game losing streak.

Jackson called himself the straw that stirs the drink when he played with the New York Yankees. Appropriately, he was the only player inducted into the Hall of Fame in 1993 when he earned 93.6 percent of the votes.

Jackson was voted to the All-Star team 14 times and finished with 563 home runs, 1,702 runs batted in, 2,584 hits, and 1,551 runs scored.

But his big moments came during the World Series. Jackson hit 10 home runs in 27 games and batted .357. He hit five home runs in the 1977 Series, including four in a row and three consecutive on the first pitch.

Despite all he accomplished, they still talk about the one he hit in Tiger Stadium.

# Which Tigers manager could Deteit best identify with— Sparky Anderson or Billy Martin?

TERRY | Billy Martin talked a big game. And he fought and scraped. But Sparky Anderson was the strange-looking guy with big ears who talked funny and won titles. He is a Detroiter, because his insecurities overshadowed his great managing skills.

Anderson was not a pretty man. We are not a pretty city. We can identify with the age lines that creep down his neck and across his face.

You know how we are. We always believe something better is coming down the road, because people often look down upon us. It was the same with Anderson, who always gave credit to players and said he always lost games and never won them.

Anderson used to tremble before games. It was a nervous reflex, because he was petrified despite managing more than 4,000 games in his career.

Anderson trembled because he always felt like the underdog. He never made it big in Major League Baseball as a player. In fact, his biggest baseball accomplishment in Detroit before winning the 1984 World Series was starring on the 1951 American Legions Championship team, which won its title at Briggs Stadium (later named Tiger Stadium).

Anderson batted .218 with 34 RBI as a second baseman for the Philadelphia Phillies in 1959. He spent the rest of his career bouncing around in the minor leagues and studied the game under manager Chuck Dressen while playing for Toronto in the International League.

After Dressen left, Anderson managed the team, and his audition got him a chance in the majors. He managed in blue-collar Cincinnati before coming to blue-collar Detroit. The Reds were a glamour team because of Pete Rose and Johnny Bench, but at their core was hustle and grit. It was the same in 1984 with Kirk Gibson, Jack Morris, and Lou Whitaker.

Anderson used a patchwork lineup and put in his best bats at the expense of defense in Detroit.

In other words Anderson won the way Detroiters made it every day. Despite our shortcomings we find a way.

DREW People cried when the Tigers fired Billy Martin on September 2, 1973, after he admitted he told his pitchers to deliberately throw at batters. It was inevitable. The team was sliding southward, and there were rumblings of altercations between Martin and his players. But that didn't matter to a lot of fans. They were upset at Martin's dismissal, because the scrappy little firebrand personified the Detroit spirit.

Martin was an underdog his entire life. Too small, too slow, but everyone underestimated his dogged determination. He always said that he only asked one thing from his players—hustle. Martin said a ballplayer didn't need talent to hustle. It only required hard work.

Detroiters loved the fact that Martin got fired in Minnesota after the 1970 season despite winning the American League West Divisional Championship because he got into a fight with one of his pitchers and

"They were upset at Martin's dismissal, because the scrappy little firebrand personified the Detroit spirit."

went out of his way to ignore the wishes of curmudgeonly Twins owner Calvin Griffith.

Martin didn't give a crap about what others thought about him, and Detroit loved that attitude. All that mattered was the bottom line, and Billy won—and won quickly. In his first year with the Tigers in 1971, Martin pushed the Tigers from a fifth-place finish in 1970 to a second-place finish. He led them to the American League East crown in 1972 where they lost to Oakland in five games.

But Martin's problem was a combustible personality that burned so brightly so quickly, it didn't take long before the flame extinguished. He didn't come to a job with emotional baggage, but a full set of luggage. But you never felt cheated with Martin. And you would go through all of the soap opera all over again and bring him back, because Billy Martin delivered. He wasn't unemployed for long—six days to be exact—before the Texas Rangers fired manager Whitey Herzog and resurrected Martin.

Q It's the bottom of the ninth, the bases are loaded with two outs, and Detroit is trailing by one. Which Tiger do you want at the plate?

TERRY | Here is my philosophy in life. If a guy has done it once, he will do it again.

Is there really a choice here? Kirk Gibson hit the most dramatic home run in our lifetime and the most important in Los Angeles Dodgers history. After leaving the Tigers, Gibson limped to the plate with a pulled left hamstring and ligament strain in his right knee in Game 1 of the 1988 World Series. The Dodgers trailed 4-3 to the Oakland A's with two outs when Gibby one-armed a two-run home run off Dennis Eckersley over the right field fence.

The A's never recovered, and the Dodgers won the Series in five.

He blasted two home runs in Game 5 of the 1984 World Series against San Diego, and his three-run shot in the eighth clinched the Tigers' first World Series championship since 1968.

And most people forget that he was Most Valuable Player in the Kansas City series that led up to the World Series. And he was the Dodgers' best player in 1988 when they beat the New York Mets in the National League Championship Series.

I never thought Gibson was a great player, but I always thought he was a great competitor. And competitors find ways to win. This guy played the game as if his pants were on fire. And we all know when there is fire, you find ways to put it out by winning games.

Was Kirk Gibson's bat strong enough to come through in a pinch?

Gibson grew up in Waterford and became an immediate fan favorite following a solid football career at Michigan State. He had a career batting average of .268 with 255 home runs, 870 RBI, and 284 stolen bases. They are not great numbers, but Gibson enjoyed great moments.

You can have the guys who hit meaningless home runs and pad their statistics. Give me the guy who wants the bat in his hand when the whole world is watching.

Gibson did it twice, which is two more times than 99 percent of Major League Baseball players.

D R E W | How could you not want the original "Hammerin' Hank" in the batter's box with the game on the line?

Hank Greenberg was money with runners in scoring position. He had the four highest single-season RBI totals in Tigers' history, including 183 in 1937. Let that number roll around in your head for a little while, Mr. Foster. Driving home 100 runs in a season is considered an All-Star-worthy season, so Greenberg pretty much had a season and a half in 1937.

You want somebody at the plate with the bases loaded who's going to make contact and not strike out. Greenberg only struck out 91 times in 619 at-bats in Greenberg's Most Valuable Player-winning 1935 season, averaging out to only one strikeout in every seven trips to the plate. That's the reliability you demand in that situation.

Greenberg was the Tigers' trailblazer. Ten years before Jackie Robinson broke the color barrier in 1945, Greenberg became baseball's first Jewish superstar. Baseball was quite comfortable in its segregation in the first half of the 20th century, and when Greenberg joined the parent club late in the 1933 season, the Tigers warned him about treading carefully. Greenberg never considered himself a boat rocker, but his quiet grace and heady play earned him acceptance from the masses. His religion became an issue in September 1934 when debate stirred about whether he would—or should—play during Rosh

Hashanah, the Jewish New Year. He compromised, playing on Rosh Hashanah, but sitting out Yom Kippur 10 days later.

Greenberg hit two home runs on Rosh Hashanah, and the Tigers beat Boston 2-1. They lost on Yom Kippur when he sat out, further confirming his value to the team. Greenberg's strong religious convictions were the inspiration for a verse from poet Edgar Guest.

> *"We shall miss him in the infield and shall miss him at the bat.*
> *"But he's true to his religion and honor him for that."*

THE BUZZ

ABOUT THE BREWS, BRATS, AND BUILDINGS

# Which rivary is better— Michigan versus Michigan State or Central Michigan versus Western Michigan?

TERRY How many times has the Michigan–Michigan State game finished with police sweeping the streets in riot gear?

Not once.

The Central Michigan–Western Michigan rivalry is easily the best in the state because the game does not end when the final gun sounds. It ends when the final guns are put away that night. OK, maybe it is not that bad. But you must admit that Chippewas and Broncos are bigger party animals than Spartans and Wolverines. After all, we attend school in Kalamazoo and Mt. Pleasant. We need more ways to vent.

The real spark began during my four-year stay as a student from 1977 to 1981. Central began traditions that have since been outlawed. We tossed toilet paper from Rose Arena following the first basket of basketball games. We were mentioned in *Playboy* magazine as the No. 13 party school in America, and we took hating Broncos to another level.

In 1978 there were rumors that some Central kids were beaten up during the CMU–WMU game in Kalamazoo. We never checked the facts and never found out if it were true. For us rumors were like stories in *The New York Times*. We went with it. The following season when the mighty Chippewas beat those dreaded Broncos 10-0 at sunny Perry-Shorts Stadium, we celebrated in the streets, threw a few bottles, and made sure the Broncos knew we were the kings of mid-major football in this state.

There are two other reasons why the Central–Western rivalry is better. We are better sports. We root for Western Michigan and Eastern Michigan to win when they are not playing Central. The Mid-American Conference is made up of mostly Ohio schools, and the last thing we felt comfortable losing to Ohio was Toledo, simply because we got the Upper Peninsula in exchange. Spartans and Wolverines would rather lose a Big Ten title than see their opponent win.

And secondly we don't bring wine and cheese to games. The closest thing we have to a blue blood is announcer Dick Enberg. Our tailgates are fun. We grill burgers and hot dogs, not glazed pheasant and veal medallions. Budweiser is our wine of choice.

And, by the way, the Chippewas were 4-0 against Western my four years there.

Of course, we watch the games sober—sometimes.

DREW   You're a little MAC daddy, Terry. So tell me—do you CMU Chippers realize that there's a game going on? If inebriation is a prerequisite for a rivalry, then the hangover state—in which Central and Western fans approach the buildup to the game and the actually playing of the game—might have a small basis for an argument.

But this isn't about who gets bragging rights for bobbing for olives in a martini trough, it's about what happens on that football field for 60 minutes. And Central and Western can't even come close. And, granted, the Spartans are often confused with a Mid-American Conference program, but their season begins and very often ends on the day they face the Wolverines.

There have been those rare occasions when the Michigan–Michigan State outcome had some bearing—albeit slight—on the national championship landscape. What's at stake with Central versus Western? The losing team pays for the winning team's bail after the victory "celebration"?

Michigan may publicly claim that Ohio State is its biggest rival, but privately, the Wolverines know that losing to the Spartans is unforgivable. They don't like losing to Ohio State, but they can't lose to Michigan State. Former Michigan coach Bo Schembechler figured that out in his first season in Ann Arbor in 1969. He had Ohio State roots, coaching under Woody Hayes, and Schembechler had pointed to the Buckeyes game at the end of the schedule on his very first day. But he lost to Michigan State in his first season, and I remember Schembechler telling me once that he was startled at the anger from alumni over the loss. From that day forward, he greatly appreciated the importance of beating Michigan State and keeping the Spartans down.

And as far as the Spartans are concerned, beating Michigan marks a successful season, even if that record were 1-10. Such a gross disproportion of perspective is all the evidence required in determining the better rivalry. So long as the Chips and Broncos drink their fill before kickoff, it doesn't really matter to either set who wins the game.

# Which Michigan school has the best college football game day experience?

TERRY

Go Blue!

OK. I made fun of veal medallions earlier. But I love them. Please don't tell my Chippewas and Broncos brothers and sisters. But I love to eat and I could stroll from tailgate to tailgate and die a happy man.

The U-M golf course tailgates put some five-star restaurants to shame. Michigan fans have some of the most innovative meals in college football. I've seen people cook venison, duck, melt-in-your-mouth steaks, and some of the wildest chicken dishes you've ever seen.

Texas boasts of its chili cookoffs. But wait until there is the first hint of chill in the air. There is enough chili at Michigan tailgates to feed a nation.

The competition does not start at kickoff. Fans are competing against each other to produce the best tasting and most innovative meals they can. And if you are not in the mood to cook, you can go to Zingerman's Deli for some of the best sandwiches and side dishes. I recommend the tuna on grilled sourdough.

The best thing is when you walk into the stadium chances are Michigan is going to win. You are packed in with more than 100,000 of your closest friends mostly because you get about 17 inches of seat to snuggle in. But once in the stadium, you get to see Michigan play in classic uniforms with the backdrop of a historic campus to the north.

This may not be the loudest stadium in the land, but people still get tingles by listening to "The Victors" fight song, watching Michigan players jump at the M Go Blue banner and being in a stadium rich with tradition.

The experience does not end after the game. After writing I love to drive downtown and eat among Michigan fans. Ann Arbor is filled with wonderful sports bars, upscale restaurants, coffee houses, and dirty spoons. People are still dressed in their Maize and Blue, talking about the game. For many game day is a near 24-hour experience. It begins at 6 a.m. in the dark on the golf course and ends with last call at the Old Town Tavern.

DREW | Go Green!
And may the spirit of Bob Ufer have mercy on my soul.

I went to Michigan, often squeezing myself into that sardine can that's Michigan Stadium. It's cool that they can brag more than 110,000 people for every home game, but I've never considered claustrophobia as a primary selling point.

The best setting is a beautiful fall afternoon in East Lansing.

Here's what you need to do, Terry. Forget using the press parking near Spartan Stadium. Find a parking spot off Hagadorn Avenue, right at the outskirts of the university, and walk to the stadium. Saunter past the dormitories where the students play a little touch football outside in between the occasional adult beverages. The students are more involved in the whole game-day experience at Michigan State than they are at Michigan.

I remember the walk to games at Michigan being more a cattle call. It was standing in traffic on the Lodge Freeway in Detroit during the afternoon rush hour, growing more frustrating with each stalled minute.

Now, I've been to my share of tailgates at both venues, and Michigan State better understands the basics—beer and brats. OK, there might be the hot dog or the occasional Italian sausage. But

Spartans fans know that if you're grilling something, it had better be contained in a membrane casing. And it creates an aroma that sweeps you off your feet and carries you the remainder of your walk to the stadium.

I'm ashamed to say this, especially because it is my alma mater, but how in the name of Vince Lombardi can any tailgate worthy of its high cholesterol allow chardonnay as a beverage? But the parking lot outside of Michigan Stadium sometimes resembles a scene from the movie *Sideways* with fans wondering if they've brought the correct pinot noir that picks up just enough of the subtleties of the special cheese they are serving.

And Michigan State fans are more inclined to stick around for the full duration of the game, regardless of the score, because they're not held hostage by the size of the crowd. As soon as Michigan fans squeeze into their little bleacher square, they're already counting the minutes before they escape soon enough to beat the dreadful traffic home.

What spirit!

> "How in the name of Vince Lombardi can any tailgate worthy of its high cholesterol allow chardonnay as a beverage?"

 # What facility best defines the Red Wings?

TERRY | Red Wings history is about grit, loose teeth, and stale beer. Nothing typifies that better than Olympia Stadium.

I used to watch games from the front row to the side of the goal with Jimmy Butsicaris, who owned the Lindell A.C. How could I not fall in love with the place when I saw smashed noses within inches of me and watched players picking up their teeth from the ice? How can you not love a place where players walked past fans to reach the dressing room? You could throw beer on Montreal Canadiens goalie Gump Worsley for heaven sakes. And who knows? He just might throw one back at you.

In the old-time arenas the sights and sounds of hockey were right in your face, no matter where your seat was located. Because of Olympia's intimacy, the blare of the horn was louder and the organ drowned out conversations. Who needs hip-hop when you could hear an organist playing "Go Wings Go" or the "Beer Barrel Polka"?

Olympia mirrored Detroit. It was not pretty. There were no bells and whistles. It was old and dingy, but there was life in the building even when it was empty.

The charm grew stronger when hockey fans were stacked on top of each other. The aisles were so steep that when you looked down on the ice from the last row, you swore that if you fell, you'd end up at center ice to break up a Production Line rush.

Remember the scene in the movie *Naked Gun* when O.J. Simpson rolled down the stairs in a wheelchair and was catapulted out of the stands? That was shot at Olympia.

DREW | Who didn't love Olympia? It wasn't part of a downtown development. Instead, it rose from an average neighborhood, like Chicago Stadium and Maple Leaf Gardens in Toronto.

But "the Joe" symbolizes the resurrection of an organization long given up for dead.

The arena was a prime reason Mike Ilitch bought the franchise from the Norris family in 1982. It was one of the first sports arenas to have luxury suites. But those seats remained virtually empty in the first years after the arena's grand opening in 1979 because there was little excitement surrounding the team.

But Ilitch had a plan: Lure the corporate dollars to fill those suites by selling the love of hockey. Once the suites sold out, he could invest the proceeds in improving the team.

That's where the renaissance began.

Joe Louis Arena became an enjoyable entertainment environment full of the amenities absent at Olympia. It offered an in-house restaurant and bar, which in the 1980s were considered state-of-the-art amenities. Once Ilitch was able to draw people down to Joe Louis Arena, the key was keeping them there. The money generated through the arena helped fund the necessary changes in building a Stanley Cup champion.

Unlike Olympia, there isn't a bad seat at Joe Louis.

That is, unless you're with the media. When the stadium was completed, its builders realized it lacked a press box. So the last two top rows of seats from four sections were removed to make room for the scribes.

Name the top three all-time radio/TV broadcasters.

No. 1: Bob Ufer—Michigan football play-by-play announcer for 37 years—was the quintessential "homer." He didn't just want Michigan to win. He sounded as though he needed Michigan to win simply to survive. He's the best, because he not only didn't mind becoming a caricature, but he actually embraced it. I remember speaking with "Ufe" during a Michigan home game during the 1981 season. I was a senior at Michigan, covering the Wolverines for *The Michigan Daily*, the student newspaper. Complications from cancer took Ufer out of the booth. He told me that his greatest compliment came from Ohio State fans, who had told him over the years how much they loved his enthusiasm despite the fact they truly despised Michigan. Ufer died from cancer not long after our conversation. Whether or not his unabashed devotion for his beloved "Meeeechigan" drove you nuts, there's no denying its entertainment value.

No. 2: Ernie Harwell—Tigers' play-by-play announcer for 42 years—was the voice of my childhood. My brother, Brian, was a huge Tigers fan and rarely missed a game on the radio. We shared a bedroom when we were smaller and sleep was a little difficult when the Tigers were on the West Coast. Brian would take his transistor radio, place it by his pillow, and pull the covers over his head. But I could still hear it.

No. 3: Dave Diles—WXYZ-TV sports anchor—was a writer masquerading as an anchor. Before the birth of ESPN and the proliferation of 24/7 cable news, local stations dedicated significant time to the sports segments of the evening news shows. They might have more than five minutes, and Diles brilliantly stretched our imaginations, weaving interesting stories along with the requisite highlights. It wasn't a surprise that Diles became a network star at ABC Sports and an accomplished author, telling Denny McLain's story.

TERRY

No. 1: Dubbed "The Ol' Announcer" by fans, Van Patrick did Tigers baseball until 1961 when he was replaced by another legend, Ernie Harwell. Patrick was the voice of the Lions from 1950 until his death in 1974. He knew how to tell a story. He was colorful, insightful, and made the Lions seem bigger than life.

Patrick had a calm and soothing voice. It was really the first announcer's voice I remember, and it seemed like a Grandpop telling sports stories to his kids when he broadcast games. He got excited when he had to be, but for the most part when Patrick spoke, it was like the entire countryside was unfolding in front of you. You could not see it. But you sure did imagine it.

No. 2: Bob Ufer was so wild about Michigan football that this list wouldn't be complete without him. Ufer wasn't a great announcer, but his passion lands him on this list.

Ufer equated coach Bo Schembechler's love for running the ball with General George Patton's prowess as a tank commander in World War II. And who can forget his elongated version of "Meeeeeechigan."

In 1979, Ufer made one of the more memorable broadcasting calls in this state's history when U-M

> "[Van Patrick's voice] seemed like a Grandpop telling sports stories to his kids when he broadcast games."

quarterback John Wangler hit Anthony Carter for a buzzer-beating 45-yard touchdown pass. The quirky announcer was practically in tears, constantly blowing his trademark touchdown horn, screaming "Thank you Fielding Yost … Thank you, Fielding Yost for that one. That was a gift from football's Vahalla!"

No. 3:   Al Ackerman was the toughest Detroit broadcaster in history. His hard-hitting commentaries practically sent smoke through the airwaves. Ackerman wasn't afraid to challenge anyone, and he never backed down. He battled Tigers president Jim Campbell, the Detroit Lions, and anyone else he believed was short-changing fans.

Ackerman's crowning moment came in 1967 when he coined the phrase "Bless You Boys" during the Tigers pennant run. The team fell short that season, but it became the battle cry the next year when the Tigers won the World Series in 1968.

Where should the potential new hockey home for the Red Wings go?

DREW | Cobo Center needs a massive expansion to compete with other convention facilities in major cities, and that would require the demolition of Joe Louis Arena.

Red Wings owner Mike Ilitch owns several acres of land in Detroit, near the Fox Theatre on Woodward Avenue. That property is used as parking for Comerica Park and Ford Field. Many people believe that's where Ilitch wants a new hockey palace, providing the finishing touch to the Foxtown sports and entertainment district.

But any new arena should remain at the riverfront—Detroit's most underused resource.

Use the Red Wings as a magnet for entertainment possibilities in a different area of downtown Detroit, instead of concentrating all of the Detroit-based professional sports teams in Foxtown.

There are several possible areas for an arena just blocks away from Joe Louis. Or why not consider Chene Park near the planned site for one of Detroit's permanent casinos?

"Use the Red Wings as a magnet for entertainment possibilities in a different area of downtown Detroit..."

TERRY | You want it on the riverfront? Are you trying to revive the city or kill it? We need foot traffic on the riverfront. We need people to enjoy that area as they do in other cities, such as Chicago.

We don't need another building to block the waterway.

Tim Springstein, an owner of Nemo's Bar & Grill in Corktown, has a great idea: Tear down Tiger Stadium and build the new arena on that site. The result would be economic growth in a historic area that already has bars and restaurants.

> "We don't need another building to block the waterway."

Don't build an arena specifically to help Mike Ilitch or the casinos. Corktown is the best plan.

The city of Detroit has sold its soul for one glorious day in sports. What would that day entail?

TERRY | This one is so easy. If the Lions won the Super Bowl, thousands of Detroit fans would die on the spot and float to heaven.

They call it Hockeytown in the winter. Some claim this is a baseball town, and people may have enjoyed themselves a bit too much during World Series celebrations in 1968 and 1984. But the federal government would have to roll into town to shut down a Lions victory celebration.

The Lions have never been to a Super Bowl, and it looks like they never will. Heck, the NFL is so convinced that the Lions won't win a Super Bowl that they brought the Super Bowl to Detroit.

They last won a NFL championship in 1957, and every player on that team remains a hero. Since that title, the Lions have won one playoff game.

That statistic is both amazing and appalling at the same time. The NFL is set up for the bumbling to do well every five years. There isn't even a word to describe how bad the Lions have been.

But that does not matter. This fan base is addicted to this team. You should see people walk into Ford Field on game days. They are dressed in Honolulu blue and silver. Their faces are painted. They are wearing hard hats and jock straps, just as if they were going to play the Packers.

The poor things look like the zombies from "Thriller" when they leave after another Lions loss. That blue face paint is now streaming down their faces with tears.

They vent on talk radio and vow on Monday and Tuesday to never watch this team play again. They throw away their Lions jerseys, curse the Ford family, and tear up their tickets.

But guess what?

By Wednesday they are at K-Mart replacing the jersey and then call the Ford Field ticket office and claim someone stole their tickets.

The Red Wings celebrations have drawn an average of one million people. I don't care if it were -15 degrees outside on Lions parade day. Every city, town, village, and hamlet would be emptied for the biggest parade in Detroit history.

DREW | Yeah, Terry, it is easy. But it's not winning the Super Bowl that would merit such a deal with the devil. If the Lions could just win the NFC championship game and book passage to the Super Bowl, it would satisfy those long-starved fans, fulfilling an unrequited dream.

The Super Bowl has grown into such a pop culture icon that the game itself is anticlimactic. Look at those teams who surprisingly got to the Super Bowl for the first time only to get annihilated. The San Diego Chargers made their maiden voyage to the game in 1995, and the Atlanta Falcons got there for the first time four years ago.

Both got blown out of the stadium by halftime, but as far as their respective fans were concerned, it was still worthy of a celebration because they finally got there and they were the object of the country's attention for two weeks.

The Lions and the St. Louis/Arizona Cardinals are the only two NFL franchises continually in existence since 1960 that haven't made it to the Super Bowl. The Lions could get to the Super Bowl and lose 40-0, and there would still be a downtown parade commemorating the achievement as soon as they returned home. The gripe isn't that they'll never win a Super Bowl, but that they'll never be good enough or lucky enough to even make the game.

It's like the Final Four in college basketball. There remain two games to win to get the national championship, but there's a tremendous sense of accomplishment in just getting to that grand stage—especially if you've never gotten there before.

# Which place was better to watch a ballgame— Tiger Stadium or Comerica Park?

TERRY | Where would you rather be—close to the action or far away?

Tiger Stadium is the choice, because you were on top of players. Yes, the pillars were annoying, but they allowed the stadium to stand more upright.

Besides the best seats were in the bleachers anyway. There were no pillars in the upper deck. They are the best seats in Detroit sports history. Fans were drenched by the sun, got a bird's-eye view of the action, and enjoyed tossing beach balls around.

I watched the Tigers clinch the 1968 pennant against the Yankees in right field with my Aunt Margo, and it felt like we were part of the celebration when the game ended. The place was packed. You could smell the stale popcorn, grilled hot dogs, and cold beer. It added to the ambiance of the stadium. It is just not watching a game, but Tiger Stadium was about touching, feeling, and grabbing the game.

It was about reaching out toward history. This was where Ted Williams, Ty Cobb, Mickey Mantle, and Babe Ruth played. This was where your dad brought you to your first game. No one talks about his or her first trip to Comerica Park. But everybody has a Tiger Stadium story about how wide eyed they were to see the old green seats and plush green grass.

These grounds were where baseball was born in our city. They are sacred. Comerica sits on an old abandoned plot of land. There is no history there.

I admit the amenities at Comerica are better. You have Tiger Court and a couple bars inside. But I go to watch games. I want to see players up close. That is why Tiger Stadium is my top choice.

D R E W | Oh, the heck with tradition. Give me sightlines that are free of those annoying pillars. It's not just about watching the game. It's about the entire experience. It's about having sufficient concession stands to get my beer quickly and having enough bathrooms to get rid of said beer quickly. If I got up to get something to eat and drink at Tiger Stadium in the first inning, I'd get back to my seat in time for the seventh-inning stretch.

It's about having well-lit and secure parking facilities across the street from the stadium rather than walking six blocks from Tiger Stadium at 11 p.m. to get back to your car.

I don't care that Babe Ruth and Lou Gehrig walked the same grounds 80 years earlier as Bobby Higginson and Dean Palmer did in the old girl's final year in 1999. History doesn't make the line go any faster when waiting to get a hot dog. I don't care if that makes me out as a modern snob.

And you know what's nice? Watching the backdrop of downtown Detroit from beyond the right field seats. It takes your attention away from the product on the field, and that's not necessarily a bad thing.

What should happen to Tiger Stadium?

DREW | Tear it down and erect a Detroit sports museum in its place.

The city of Detroit and Tigers owner Mike Ilitch blew this one when they arranged a deal for Ilitch to handle the daily maintenance of the old stadium upon the Tigers' departure to Comerica Park for the 2000 season. It should have been preserved as a shrine to this city's rich baseball tradition. How cool would it have been to have Tiger Stadium serve as the site for the 2005 Home Run Derby during the All-Star Week festivities? How inspiring could it have been to have young kids play on the same grounds that were once graced by the footsteps of Babe Ruth and Joe DiMaggio?

But the stadium's only use in the last six years was as a movie prop—the reincarnation of Yankee Stadium circa 1961 for Billy Crystal's cinematic ode to Roger Maris's epic chase of the Bambino's single-season home run record in *61**.

But once the production crews departed in 2002, the old stadium died of neglect.

It's ridiculous keeping the stadium up in its current state. It remains a cherished memory, but there's another way to pay homage to the history of that locale.

Build a museum that could house artifacts that are special to the Detroit sports conscience, and I guarantee you that fathers would love spending a weekend afternoon there with their sons, reminiscing about some of the events that they attended in person when they were younger. Sports is one of the stronger generational bonds in Detroit.

The museum could also serve as the new home for the Michigan Sports Hall of Fame, getting it out of Cobo Hall and placing it in a setting more reflective of the history that the organization represents.

You don't need more apartment lofts there. Everybody's building places to live downtown while forgetting to add the necessary elements to residential life such as grocery stores and drugstores. I'm all for constructing magnets that will pull people into the city for things they can't necessarily get out in the suburbs, and a sports museum on the former grounds of their childhood ballpark satisfies that objective.

TERRY | We must figure a way to incorporate the integrity of Tiger Stadium into the new Joe Louis Arena. Corktown needs a sure-fire draw to the bars and restaurants that were abandoned when the Tigers moved down the road to Comerica Park.

Red Wings owner Mike Ilitch owes it to his old neighbors. This area bustled on Tigers' game days. The bars and restaurants were filled. People strolled the streets, and the ballpark-bound fans provided homeowners with pocket change by parking in their lots and backyards.

Eventually the Joe Louis Arena on the riverfront must be torn down to accommodate the Cobo Center expansion. We are losing large conventions to other cities because Cobo must be expanded another 400,000 square feet to keep the auto show and other big shows.

The best plan is to expand toward the river, which could threaten Joe Louis Arena.

If that happens, the new JLA must move to Corktown. I know Ilitch wants that new arena behind the Fox Theater. But perhaps it is time to share the wealth with the rest of downtown.

The folks in Corktown are all for it. The next time you go into Nemo's, ask the owners about the idea. They love it.

It is a perfect location. There is plenty of room to not only build an arena but perhaps add a few shops, condos, and restaurants.

Sorry, Drew. A sports museum would draw flies. People would rush to see it initially, but then attendance would dry up. Do people really care enough about the top athletes in Michigan where they would pay money to see a few plaques, uniforms, and jock straps?

We don't even have enough people going to the art museums downtown.

Now if you put the Red Wings down there, that could be a different story.

# What was the best feature of Tiger Stadium?

DREW | How could you not love the fact that Tiger Stadium was part of a residential neighborhood, similar to Wrigley Field on Chicago's North Side?

That was its greatest charm. Yeah, you had the right field overhang that created the illusion of being close enough to tap the pitcher on the back as he stood on the mound.

But you want to talk about intimacy?

Go across Michigan Avenue and traverse a couple blocks down Trumbull Avenue, and you'll see the owners of the homes in that area offering choice parking on their lawns for $20. That's what was passed off as VIP parking in the days when ballparks weren't vast entertainment meccas—restaurants and massive parking facilities all tied together.

It was the neighborhood bar, the neighborhood pool hall, the neighborhood "five and dime," and, oh by the way, walk across the street and you can catch the Tigers and the Yankees on a warm summer afternoon.

It wasn't in downtown Detroit. It was in a little insulated community called Corktown. Families grew up in the shadows of Major League Baseball. You walk through the neighborhoods leading to Tiger Stadium, and you'd wonder if this was what it was like walking through the Brooklyn neighborhoods on your way to Ebbets Field.

TERRY | They ruined Tiger Stadium when they removed the green wooden seats for plastic blue and orange seats. The ambience of the stadium changed forever. The green wooden seats were perfect for this relic of a ballpark.

First of all they made Tiger Stadium more intimate. The stadium seemed to topple over the field. It was an old-school touch that never should have changed.

And secondly the Tigers enjoyed more of a home-field advantage.

People used to raise and slam the green seats while crying for a Tiger rally, and they made the loudest racket. There was no sweeter sound than listening to thousands of Tigers fans scream, "We want a hit!" while pounding on those noisy chairs. It sometimes sounded like a rickety locomotive streaming down a railroad track.

It was even louder on bat day, because half the crowd slammed their bats while the other half slammed their seats.

Sadly, the seats began to give way to weather and the slamming and were replaced with more durable plastic seats. The old lady was never the same. The Tigers took notice. Although the seats at Comerica are made of plastic, most are green.

When the stadium closed, fans only wanted two things. They wanted a piece of sod and dirt. And then they grabbed the green seats. I cannot tell you how many backyard picnics I've been to where owners proudly show off their green Tiger Stadium seats.

Oh, and I forgot to mention one other thing. Few people saw one of the best parts of Tiger Stadium. It was the sign that hung outside the visitors clubhouse.

It read, "Visitors Clubhouse. No visitors."

 # After Detroit, what is the best sports city in the state of Michigan?

TERRY | I am sitting in a hotel room right now in Michigan's next best sports center. The high rollers in Grand Rapids worked hard the last 20 years to make it a mini sports mecca.

I am just down the street from Van Andel Arena, which is the nicest arena in the state outside of The Palace. This $70-million complex holds 10,843 spectators, and the Grand Rapids Griffins hockey team enjoyed season ticket sales as high as 7,000.

The Pistons and Michigan State play basketball games here. It is home to the Grand Rapids Rampage of the Arena Football League and the NCAA routinely hosts NCAA hockey championships at Van Andel.

Just outside of town in Comstock Park sits Fifth/Third Ball Park, home to the Grand Rapids Whitecaps. This 6,000-seat stadium is one of the models of modern-day minor league parks. It has comfortable seating, a picnic area, and grassy knoll to enjoy the game.

Drew, the only game that counts for you is baseball. So let me roll some numbers by you. The Whitecaps broke Class A attendance records their first four years and they became the fourth fastest minor league franchise to get two million fans through the turnstiles.

The Whitecaps have spurred economic development on the north side of town. Fast food joints, sports bars, and big box stores opened up soon afterward.

Downtown Van Andel helped spur a sluggish downtown. Now people go to games and then walk to The B.O.B, Sierra Room, Taps, and TGI Friday's.

I almost forgot the high schools. The *Grand Rapids Press* provides more than two full pages of coverage on prep hoops and football, making games huge events. Places like Rockford and Grandville draw more than 6,000 people to games. The area also boosts national champion Grand Valley in football, and Calvin and Hope is one of the best Division III rivalries in the country.

This place is so much fun that we could enjoy a sports weekend here almost as easily as we could in Detroit.

D R E W | It's only appropriate that you used the baseball analogy, ol' shiny-headed one, because you're stuck in left field on this one.

It's not even close. Just follow the pulsating rhythms northward on I-75 about 50 miles north of Detroit and you'll find the heartbeat of high school basketball in the state of Michigan—Flint, baby—Flint!

Grand Rapids has become a minor league sports haven, but the passion doesn't register a blip on the sports Richter scale when compared to a high school Friday night back in the day when Flint Northwestern went up against Flint Central or Flint Northern battled Flint Beecher. The personal connection isn't there with the minor league teams because there isn't a community alliance like there is with high school sports.

And you know, Terry, from your years of covering high school sports that few things captivate the little to midsize communities more than that special prep team or player. It creates more of a bond.

These athletes are just passing through Grand Rapids on their way to hopefully more prominent careers. But the great Flint high school basketball players always remain part of Flint wherever else their careers might take them. And they remain a tremendous source of local pride even as the depressed auto economy renders Flint into a hallowed out relic.

Why don't you engage me with the honor roll of the great minor league basketball and hockey players who once used Grand Rapids as a pit stop?

This book isn't big enough to incorporate all of the big guns from Flint, so I'll just give you the all-time starting five—Trent Tucker, Glen Rice, Jeff Grayer, Mateen Cleaves, and Roy Marble. Each remains a legend at their respective schools and a source of motivation for their young legacies.

The population numbers in Flint have progressively decreased in relation to the jobs lost from General Motors' reduced influence in the town over the years, but the high school gyms on winter Friday evenings remain on jam. And that's indicative of a passionate sports town. Basketball is the great escape for Flint, a chance to temporarily put aside the thoughts of a dying economy and hang tightly onto what made them alive.

 # The Grand Prix has been held in downtown and on Belle Isle. Which was better?

DREW The drivers hated the street course. The turns were too tight, prohibiting them from reaching the speeds they desired. There wasn't enough passing room for their tastes. But the bottom line was the European drivers who came here for the Formula One version of the race didn't want to be in Detroit. It wasn't cosmopolitan enough for their pretentiousness. But I still maintain that race provided some of the best public relations for the city, because the downtown track allowed you to actually see the city on television. Yeah, it had its blemishes, which some of the more pompous Formula One drivers like Frenchman Alain Prost took great delight in criticizing. (Yeah, like the French have any justification in belittling the character of others.)

It was more of a party downtown than it was at Belle Isle, but what's wrong with that? Isn't the real attractiveness of the major sports event the ancillary activities? The Grand Prix was promoted as a celebration even though Detroit doesn't fit the champagne and caviar set of Formula One. The affairs held on downtown rooftops on race day were cool. It didn't matter that most of the attendees probably couldn't identify a single driver. It was a happening, something that helped Detroit stand apart from the pack—if only for a few hours on a summer afternoon. It's too bad that race organizers backed down and moved the race to Belle Isle—a logistical nightmare considering that the sole access to the site was a bridge. It made the race more of a public inconvenience than any difficulties that might have emerged when it was downtown.

TERRY | The question is do you like racing or do you like to party? The Belle Isle course reminded racers of Monte Carlo. Both courses were near the water and actually allowed people to race. The Belle Isle course featured three long straight-aways, and was quicker and more exciting.

And how about this concept?

People could actually see the race. If you got the right spot you could eye-ball three or four different spots on the track. Fans could move around and check out the pit area or one of the hairpin turns.

Boodini, did you actually consider the concept of people paying their money to watch an actual race?

Downtown you paid to see buildings and an occasional whiz of color. Now who pays money to get a close-up of downtown Detroit? The tourists sure don't.

Downtown was a great party venue and place to people watch. I loved hanging down there checking out the Brazilian babes. But it was not a good place to view the race. The downtown course was bumpy and slow, and created too many disruptions. I also hated the way drivers dogged Detroit. The late, great Ayrton Senna and Alaine Prost took such glee in pointing out the blemishes of downtown. These guys were so eager to get out of town they had their private jets warming up during the final laps of the race.

Perhaps I am the wrong guy to answer this question. I lived downtown during the early downtown Grand Prix, and it was nearly impossible for me to get home. Every street was closed, and you had to take busses to work. And if you were lucky, the bus might drop you off within four blocks of where you were trying to go. So I left the office bitter and got home ready to punch somebody.

 # Could Detroit host a Summer Olympics?

TERRY | If Mexico City can host an Olympics, then so can Detroit. People mistakenly think Olympics are only held in glamour cities that are finished products. I can tell you that neither Atlanta nor Athens was a finished product when it held the Olympics.

Detroit is one of the most passionate sports places in the world, and we already have venues that can host Olympics. Our area will get a second dry run in 2008 when it plays host to its second junior Olympic Games. There won't be as many people, but the junior Olympics prove Detroit has the facilities to host an Olympic Games.

Can you imagine 112,000 people jammed inside an upgraded Michigan Stadium for opening and closing ceremonies? Michigan State has a nice outdoor pool facility. The Palace, Joe Louis Arena, Crisler Arena, and Breslin can host basketball, wrestling, and gymnastics. We could have weight-lifting and boxing at the Fox Theater.

We have the facilities to host any Olympic event in the world. Of course we'd have to build an Olympic rowing facility on Belle Isle and would have to upgrade the Velodrome for biking on Detroit's east side.

The problem is where do you put all these people? Detroit lacks enough hotel space. But permanent casinos with hotels are on the way, and thank goodness we have the river. The Detroit River can line up cruise ships on the Detroit and Windsor side. You can even park them up in Port Huron, Traverse City, and Bay City for out state events.

Detroit is building condos and apartments in the old Cass Corridor and Brush Park. There are two Olympic villages for the athletes and the media right there.

It can be done. We've already hosted Super Bowl XL, and the 2009 Final Four is on its way. Those events are not as big as the Olympics, but they are pretty major events.

Heck, I am so fired up now let's stop talking about bringing the Olympics. Put me on the Detroit Olympic Committee right now.

D R E W | Terry, perhaps you need to lie down and take a little nap because your judgment is clouding up here down the homestretch.

Not only could it never happen, but there's no way Detroit could even submit a reasonable bid with the International Olympic Committee for consideration.

Where's the open-air stadium required by IOC rules for the opening and closing ceremonies? Michigan Stadium is certainly big enough, and there's the possibility of refurbishing the facility to incorporate the track-and-field competition logistics, but there's no way the IOC would approve having the main stadium 45 minutes away from the games' central location. And you're certainly not going to build such a single purpose facility for this area just for the Olympics.

And you need a respectable mass transit system to help move the massive flow of humanity around the area with as little clogging as possible. You were in Atlanta, Terry, in 1996. You know it was an absolute joke with transportation. And Atlanta had a light-rail system. If they couldn't pull it off without causing enormous headaches, how do you expect Detroit to make it work with the People Mover?

Here's a novel concept? Why not invest a tenth of the begging-for-bankruptcy costs of putting on this spectacle into upgrading the city's infrastructure? You want a Detroit Olympics? Why not encourage the public school system to compete and thrive to become a gold medal-worthy operation?

The Super Bowl is all that this city can handle, and some might consider that a stretch.

Name the top three all-time Detroit sports bars to watch a game if you don't have tickets.

TERRY | **No. 1:** Lindell A.C. in Detroit. The granddaddy of all Detroit sports bars is no longer with us. But the legend lives on. This was one of the final places where sports stars from all over the city gathered after games to mingle with fans. You not only could come and watch games on one of three television sets, but you might be sitting next to Lions linebacker Wayne Walker or lineman Alex Karras. It was not spectacular. It was a wood-paneled, smoky place that crammed 144 chairs together.

This was where the 1968 Tigers came to celebrate after winning the pennant over the New York Yankees. They finally closed the place down, and players poured drinks for free.

The Lindell served the best burgers in town. The walls were decorated with mostly black and white photos that acted as a historical walk through Detroit's rich sports past. And everyone talked about Walker's jock strap, which hung by the jukebox. Another reason why it was my favorite place is because my mother, Betty, worked there for 20 years, and I worked weekends during my school days at Cass Tech.

I once served WWF wrestler Andre the Giant four third-pound burgers, and he wolfed them down as if they were a sack of White Castles.

It was a place to meet people of all walks of life both famous and ordinary. The granddaddy is no longer with us. But the memories remain a part of Detroit sports lore. Nemo's is great, and it would be on my list if not for my Lindell ties.

243

No. 2: Rosie O'Grady's in Clinton Township. There are no strangers here. A young man used to stop at Rosie's, because he did not have cable television and loved to watch the Tigers. Rosie's hired him as a bouncer and sat him by one of the big screen televisions so he could earn a little money and check out his favorite ball team.

They welcome you with hospitality and stun you with superior food that includes gigantic burgers, pizza, and Nathan's authentic hot dogs. I love the mafia table where you can sit 10 people in the corner. It gives you a bird's-eye view of the dance floor. Rosie's also has a backroom filled with television sets for private parties.

Check out my girls, Julie, Teri, and Patty. And if you are nice, Teri will strike a Heisman pose just for the heck of it.

How will you know them? You just will. That is the lure of Rosie's. You are a stranger the first time you walk through the door. You are a friend the second time.

I know you love Checker Bar and Mr. Joe's, Drew. That's only because you never venture to the west side of town.

Make a trip. You might change your mind.

No. 3: Malarkeys in Southgate. It is possible to enjoy the perfect sporting experience here alone or with the boys.

Go in on a Saturday afternoon for college football games. Order the breadsticks and a brew. Watch a couple of games and before dinner order the steak bits, which are to die for, and check out the late games. By the time those games end, the place is filled with beautiful women ready to dance.

There are pool tables and dartboards in the back. But I never venture that far. The bar is a great place for people watching and checking out the big games. We started going there for radio appearances, which got bigger and better. It was so much fun we did not want to leave. The wait staff is beautiful, and it is a nice casual place perfect for dates or solo excursions.

And by the way, Drew. The burgers and pickles are better there than at Mr. Joe's. Once again you need to get out of the neighborhood a little more.

DREW | **No. 1:** Nemo's—Corktown in Detroit. Baseball's Opening Day is a high holy day in Detroit, and if Tiger Stadium was the cathedral, then this little bar sitting kittie-corner from the stadium on Michigan Avenue was the neighborhood church. A caravan of four made the pilgrimage on Opening Day 1981. My three friends and I didn't have tickets to the ballgame. Our plan was to experience the day from Nemo's. The bar opened at 8 a.m., but getting a spot inside the bar required getting in line no later than 7 a.m. It was a wild day that didn't end until we left around 9 p.m. We didn't even know who won the ballgame. It didn't matter. Nemo's is No. 1, because it embodies Detroit sports.

No. 2: Checker Bar in downtown. The best seat in town was at the bar of this long-standing Detroit establishment. The Checker satisfied the lunchtime appetites of many businessmen. There was a simple charm to the environment. There was only one television at the bar. You didn't need any extra distractions from the classic cheeseburger. It's all about the grilled onions, baby. It provided a gentle sweetness that perfectly balanced the tartness of the old dill pickle chips. When the *Free Press* first hired me to freelance for them in September 1992, I walked over to my father's office at Cadillac Tower to give him the news. He took me out to lunch for a burger and a brew at the Checker.

No. 3: Mr. Joe's in Southfield. I first discovered this Southfield tavern in the fall of 1983 when a *Free Press* coworker, a Philadelphia native, and I decided to take the afternoon off and find a place that was televising the Phillies' playoff game. The burgers were excellent, but even better was that they let you apply the amount of condiments. *And... I... love... pickles!* They practically give you a jar of them. It got to the point on future visits when the waitress would ask if I wanted a little cheeseburger to go with my pickle sandwich.

There are plenty of televisions in order to watch plenty of different games, but you've got to love a place that gives you such control over your food.